PANDERING AND PUNDITRY

An Election Year Journal

Kirk D. Sinclair, PhD

I0102744

© Kirk D. Sinclair 2025

All rights reserved.

No parts of this manuscript may be copied and shared without permission and attribution to the author.

Author's website: www.unenlightenedwisdom.com

ISBN: 979-8-9930279-0-6

Library of Congress Control Number: 2025918935

First Edition, 2025

This is a publication of the **Unenlightened Wisdom Project**. For an overview of this ten year endeavor see the project's White Paper, available from the author's website.

TABLE OF CONTENTS

INTRODUCTION: Election Campaigns and Health Outcomes

I kept a journal during the 2024 election year to supplement the beginning of the *Unenlightened Wisdom Project.*[1] Over the next ten years the project covers a logical sequence of practicalities beginning with living well for our brain health and ending with direct participation in democracy. Election campaigns feature pandering that conforms voters to groupthink, along with punditry that analyzes the effectiveness of the pandering. Indeed, "campaigning" is a suitable synonym for political pandering … or corporate marketing. This 2024 election year journal provides context needed for the pursuit of collective wisdom over the pandering and punditry that reinforces groupthink.

Our country ranks near the bottom in terms of Alzheimer's and dementia deaths, with only seven countries ranked lower.[2] We are, by far, the worst country in the world in terms of deaths from drug abuse.[3] On the "bright side," for life expectancy we manage to rank 48th,[4] though that is still worse than most advanced countries. Election campaigns do not focus on comparative health outcomes, even though our economics, politics and culture contribute to why we fare badly in comparison to other countries. Campaigns seldom challenge the status quo of our social systems, hence they will not avert our projected slide further down in life expectancy relative to other countries, falling to 66th by the year 2050.[5]

Election year campaigns focus more on consumer issues such as inflation and taxes, or on macroeconomic indicators such as the stock market, GDP or national deficit. Few Americans realize that we are the most overworked developed nation in the world,[6] but you will never hear this comparison made during an election campaign. The quality and quantity of work conditions impact health outcomes in large measure.

For obvious reasons, our election campaigns never challenge our two party political system where "winner takes all." Despite the countries with better health outcomes having multiple parties and coalition governments, third party attempts in this country are discouraged during election campaigns by the two entrenched parties. With this and most other issues the two parties resort to pandering with fear and anger, claiming that anything undermining their own influence or ideology will allow the other party to ruin the country. This elevated fear and anger undermines our emotional and brain health.

---

[1] The website for The Unenlightened Wisdom Project is https://www.unenlightenedwisdom.com/
[2] *Alzheimer's and Dementia Death Rate per 100,000 Age Standardized* (2020). World Life Expectancy. Retrieved from https://www.worldlifeexpectancy.com/cause-of-death/alzheimers-dementia/by-country/
[3] *Drug Use Death Rate per 100,000 Age Standardized* (2020). World Live Expectancy. Retrieved from https://www.worldlifeexpectancy.com/cause-of-death/drug-use/by-country/
[4] *Life Expectance of the World Population* (2024). Worldometer. Retrieved from https://www.worldometers.info/demographics/life-expectancy/#countries-ranked-by-life-expectancy
[5] *Life expectancy by country in 2050* (2024). Database Earth. Retrieved from https://database.earth/population/life-expectancy/2050.
[6] Miller, G.E. (2025). *The U.S. is the Most Overworked Developed Nation in the World.* 20 Something Finance. From https://20somethingfinance.com/american-hours-worked-productivity-vacation/

The entrenchment of both our economic and political systems ultimately results from the judicial review authority the Supreme Court gave itself.[7] The 2024 election highlighted the 50 year precedent of Roe vs Wade being overturned, but ignored as usual the Supreme Court jurisprudence that led to corporation personhood,[8] and money as free speech.[9] No election campaign, and extremely few political pundits, will point out the fact that the unelected branch of government with no term limits has ultimate authority over the other two branches, an authority they bestowed upon themselves.

The Enlightenment, also called the Age of Reason, embraced ideals like individualism and materialism. Neuroscience demonstrates that both ideals undermine the physiology that maintains brain health, while ethnographers discovering nomadic tribes with no previous civilized contact confirm that individualism and materialism were not natural desires. Spurred by corporate funded think tanks and corporate funded chairs of academic departments, our economic and political systems take these ideals to a further extreme than other advanced countries with better health. A remedy to this Enlightenment induced fog will not come from the status quo that benefits from the current philosophy and systems in place.

All of the entries except for the final one were crafted before the election, some while Biden was still the candidate, though some polishing and insertion of citations continued afterwards. Part One of this journal presents contextual background from my observations as someone who lives in the same house where I was raised. Part Two applies this contextual background to the prominent campaign issues of 2024. Part Three suggests requirements for applying collective wisdom in the future to the systemic problems revealed by the 2024 election year. The final entry serves as a post mortem recap on the 2024 election as a confirmative illustration of previous entries.

---

[7] *Marbury v. Madison*. 5 U.S. 137 (1803). U.S. Supreme Court.
[8] *Santa Clara County v. Southern Pacific Railroad Co*. 118 U.S. 394 (1886). U.S. Supreme Court.
[9] *Buckley v. Valeo*. 421 U.S. 1 (1986). U.S. Supreme Court.

PART ONE: Contextual Understanding

Entry #1: Candidates Then and Now

When I was six years old my parents showed me pictures of John F. Kennedy and Richard M. Nixon and asked which one would get my "vote" for President. My mother was a Democrat and my father was a Republican, but neither pressured me to pick their favored candidate. Both JFK at age 43 and Nixon at age 47 looked old to me, but I chose the younger looking JFK because looks matter for a six year old. Sixty-four years later and we are slated to choose between two Presidential candidates who are now 77 and 81. My six year old self would be disgusted!

We gain wisdom from vetting a diversity of experiences. I vetted some of my wisdom from experiences as a long term caregiver for three different relatives with dementia. I supplement that by vetting experiences as an academic to research both brain health and cognitive decline. Based upon these experiences, along with observing videos of Biden and Trump, I conclude that both Presidential candidates show cognitive decline. Superficial looks may matter to a six year old, but I believe even at that age I would have been swayed by their apparent mental capacities. Now the mental capacity of a candidate does not seem to matter even for adults.[10]

We are more conscientious about ageism these days and that is a good thing. Those whom we call superagers maintain vibrant brain health well into their nineties.[11] A mildly declining octogenarian may yet surpass the cognitive function of many people in their forties, but whether that might be true for either current candidate is doubtful. One factor preventing people from superaging is stress, and the President has a stress laden responsibility. Chronic stress can turn mild cognitive decline into dementia, with the elderly particularly vulnerable. Even if the candidates had not shown any signs of cognitive decline previously, they have a heightened chance of dementia before their term of office concludes. This should generate concern for both the nation and the candidates themselves.

As a full time home caregiver going on fifteen years, I apply the oxygen mask principle for my loved one. If you are a parent on an airplane you put your oxygen mask on first, as motivated as you might be to save the life of your child above all else. You cannot best take care of others unless you first take care of yourself. An elderly person cannot be the best choice for running the country unless immunized from the ravages of stress, a virtually impossible condition for an elderly President of the United States, unless he/she is psychopathic.

I continue to live in the house where my parents asked me to "vote" as a six year old, but I never became affiliated with either party. My parents tolerating their party differences allowed me to see that neither party was all wrong nor all right. This may have begun my journey as a lifelong

---

[10] These online journal entries for *Election Campaign Wisdom* began months before the fateful Presidential debate of June 27, 2024.

[11] Northwestern Medicine (2023, October). *4 Habits of Superagers*. Healthbeat Newsletter.

skeptic, a crucial ingredient for acquiring wisdom. Unfortunately, two people with different party affiliations are not as likely to be tolerant of each other now, nor apply any skepticism to their own party. This is another difference between then and now, between a time when we chose between forty somethings and a time when we seem unconcerned about voting an elderly man into arguably the most stressful job in the country,

This election year journal starts with providing contextual background for the ways in which economics, politics and culture has changed or stayed the same, from the perspective of one who has remained in the same rural village throughout. Most important will be the background on how misinformation and news reporting has changed between then and now, a key factor in why people from different parties avoid being with each other, and why we have lowered the bottom in regards to the politicians and political parties we support.

Entry #2: The Flip and Shift

In addition to the respect my parents had for each other's party preference, allowing me to see that neither was all right nor all wrong, two other factors that made me a confirmed unaffiliate all my life were the flip and shift. That is to say, the parties often flipped their views during my lifetime, while what was considered the political center has shifted. As a devout skeptic I do not give my allegiance to something that cannot be pinned down; I suggest the same for you.

As for the shift of center, or what is considered moderate, the same economic policies that once branded President and General Dwight Eisenhower as a moderate now brands Senator Bernie Sanders as a progressive radical by mainstream media. A certain amount of changing with the times should be expected, but another shift in the decades since Eisenhower has been the relentlessly expanding wealth disparity. These two shifts of ideology and wealth disparity are no mere coincidence.

Eisenhower and Sanders share similar concerns about the military-industrial complex. General Eisenhower, in confidential documents compiled and made public several decades later in the book **Hiroshima"s Shadow**,[12] advised against the dropping of the atom bomb, noting that Japan already had offered terms of surrender. The saving of American military lives was a political red herring that reveals the most consequential moral and health issue, over which the parties have flipped.

During Eisenhower's time if you were against the dropping of the bomb you were statistically more likely to be a Republican; now you are more likely to be a Democrat. Regardless of how you feel either way, or the reasons why, this is not an issue that should flip over time. This issue alone provides a testament to how both parties place politics over principle, and the influence they have to conform followers towards groupthink.

---

[12] Bird, K. & Lifschultz, L. (1998). *Hiroshima's Shadow*. Pamphleteer's Press.

Over the decades there have been many flips by both parties and individual politicians. An individual could be flipping to buck the party line due to a refreshing change of conscience, but entire parties flipping usually reflect a change in strategy to win over voters … or to distract them. Some of these flips provide worthy material for "then and now" topics in this election year journal.

Chances are if you are devoted in your views, whether Democrat or Republican, conservative or liberal, you already sense and disapprove of where my political skepticism is heading. Be aware that wisdom requires an expanding diversity of experiences from which to filter. A skeptic believes that no ideology is either all right or all wrong, but rather offers something that enhances your journey through life.

Entry #3: Economics Then and Now

I live in the house where I was raised. Middle to lower middle class households lived on my street while I was growing up; now middle to upper middle class households occupy the same structures, with some of them being second homes. My father had a GED as the lone wage earner supporting a family of five sons. My wife Cindy and I supported our family of two daughters and one son with two combined incomes. Between us we have a PhD, two Masters, two professional certifications and three Bachelor degrees.

My father acquired a home that cost twice his annual salary as a specialty advertising salesman, paid for with a thirty year mortgage. When I purchased the home from my brothers at a 40% discount, during the downturn in the housing market that occurred in the early nineties, the cost still was three times our combined incomes as professionals. All my father's sons went to college without being saddled with student debt; our kids are projected to be paying down student loan debt well into their future.

We live in a small town with a population nearly the same for centuries, in a state noted as "the land of steady habits." As a kid I could go a few hundred yards to get tootsie rolls or ammo for my toy cap gun from a neighborhood business, or a sundae and comic books from the local drug store. The local grocery and hardware stores provided almost everything our family needed. Now every one of those small businesses are gone.

These local trends correlate with a national shift towards a corporate economy and a trend of wealth disparity steadily increasing for decades. Wealth disparity is an indicator for both causes and effects that disadvantage the middle class and small businesses. Wealth disparity increased since the sixties with both Democratic and Republican administrations, both Democratic and Republican Congresses, whether the branches of government were split between parties or united. Corporate funding of think tanks such as the Cato Institute and interest groups such as the US Chamber of Commerce have increased steadily as well, as did corporate campaign contributions to the two political parties.

Fifteen years ago I published a work titled: **Systems out of Balance: How Misinformation Hurts the Middle Class**.[13] "Systems" refers to our economic, political and cultural systems. "Out of Balance" refers to trends such as wealth disparity that never reverse, or maintain "balance." The "balance" of natural systems is called homeostasis, maintained by feedback from the environment. In social systems this feedback is provided by the news being provided. The irreversible trends from being out of balance means the feedback in our society amounts to misinformation, such as with the news that corporate funded think tanks and interest groups provide.

Systems out of Balance only described how social systems work. This nagged at me, like I was one of those people who just like to complain without offering alternatives. Soon after publication I became a full time caregiver for Cindy, afflicted with early onset Alzheimer's. I abandoned all publicity and marketing as I turned my full attention and research towards caring for my wife and learning about brain health.

From studies of superagers I learned that lifestyle factors good for the brain also benefit society, and that misinformation which throws society out of balance also undermines brain health. If I could rewrite the subtitle for my earlier work I would claim: "How Misinformation Hurts Us All," and make the book prescriptive as well as descriptive. Instead, I began the ten year _Unenlightened Wisdom Project_, in part as an endeavor to preserve my own brain health as a caregiver. These journal entries contribute to that project.

Entry #4: Community Then and Now

There are eleven houses and one small apartment complex on my street. In my first eighteen years growing up two out of the eleven households here changed occupants once, the rest remained the same. Over the next 52 years the households changed occupants 34 times, with every house except ours changing occupants at least once. I am the only remaining occupant on my street since the time of my birth.

This makes me unique in transient American society. Moving statistics provided by moveBuddha[14] cites our frequency of moving as 11.7 times per lifetime, which works out to a little less than once every seven years. Telling anybody I live in the house where I was raised elicits amazed and congratulatory comments.

This transiency contributes to a phenomenon Robert Putnam documents in his book, **Bowling Alone**.[15] Community involvement has decreased over time, while social isolation has increased. One criticism of Putnam's thesis is that volunteerism has increased, but such a change in

---

[13] Sinclair, K. (2009). _Systems out of Balance: How Misinformation Hurts the Middle Class_. Mill City Press.
[14] Carrigan, R. (2025, Feb). _Moving Industry Statistics_. moveBuddha. From https://www.movebuddha.com/blog/moving-industry-statistics/
[15] Putnam, R. (2001). _Bowling Alone_. Simon & Schuster.

volunteerism actually reflects our transitory nature. People volunteering for organizations like the Peace Corps increase, while volunteers for community improvement projects decrease. Soup kitchens have increased, potluck suppers have decreased.

When we walked across the country to reboot Cindy's life and brain health I witnessed first hand the decrease in the village hubs that served as gathering places for neighborhoods.[16] In Missouri I listened to the lament of closing small town post offices; in Indiana the lament of disappearing general stores; in West Virginia the lament of school consolidation. We are a nation increasingly keeping to ourselves … or turning to interest groups to fill the social void of village hubs.

I still consider my street to be neighborly, while our town still has village hubs for gathering. We call out greetings to each other from our porches and help each other after snowstorms. Before Cindy's affliction, we invited neighbors over for dinner and they invited us over in return. For Christmas, Cindy baked her famous cinnamon bread to give out to neighbors, while I had the hard job of delivering the bread and being invited in for hot chocolate and cookies. After Cindy's early onset dementia, neighbors assisted my role as her full time caregiver.

Like the bar in Cheers, everybody knows your name in this neighborhood, but even here our neighborly care comes with a bit more privacy. There were no fences between houses throughout my childhood; now there are seven. Kids are not gallivanting up and down the street as frequently. Our sloped yard used to be a gathering place for sledding and then snowboarding, but not in over a decade. There were no tablets or smartphones commanding the attention of kids as they stayed homebound.

As I filter through the social media on my own iPad I cringe at the impact the new technology is having on both youth and adults. It's one thing to be socially isolated, it's quite another to be stewing on fear, anger and entitlement while living in relative isolation. Of all the factors that have undermined our social fabric between then and now, "social" media has one of the greatest impacts, perhaps surpassed only by the changes in news media over the decades.

Entry #5: Media Then and Now

"Ask not what your country can do for you. Ask what you can do for your country."

Those words from President Kennedy remain the most stirring declaration from a President in my lifetime. Unfortunately, news media during the sixties framed every politician's words and actions in terms of impact on voters. Seemingly, none of our elected officials were capable of doing something purely for the sake of the country without taking into account how their own political careers might be affected, not the kind of leadership that inspires citizens to heed Kennedy's words.

---

[16] The account of our walk across the country and my ongoing caregiver journey is at https://www.humanityhiker.com/

Was such cynicism true some of the time? Sure. Was this true for every politician all of the time? Only in the cynical eyes of mainstream punditry. Even so, the sixties were the highpoint in my lifetime for news media reporting. The changes since then from decentralized reporting to centralized news punditry profoundly impacted the other "then and now" changes to our social systems.

In the sixties my local print media consisted of the Winsted Citizen and Hartford Courant. Our broadcast media viewing consisted of a half hour of local news followed by a half hour of CBS News with Walter Cronkite. Most of the news reporting was based on investigative journalism. Since much of the news formats were local, so was much of the investigative journalism. This increased the chances and occurrences of newsworthy events being investigated, along with a diversity of biases from which they would be covered.

The seventies began with the 1971 Powell Memorandum to the US Chamber of Commerce[17] calling for corporations to essentially market their image and ideology to the most influential segments of society.[18] This caused a burgeoning of lobbyists and interest groups. The interest groups known as think tanks provided pundits for news media coverage.

The eighties began with the first 24 hour news station. The amount of investigative journalism did not increase; news talk shows filled in the time with hosts and guests giving their opinions. Later in the eighties the FCC abolished the Fairness Doctrine that required both sides of important public issues to be presented on government licensed airwaves.[19] In addition to owning media sources, for profit corporations with much greater resources could similarly be one-sided with free speech protections.

The nineties witnessed a great consolidation of media. The appeals to Congress of struggling local media were ignored while legislation passed to help corporations in the changing media landscape. Sinclair Broadcasting Group in particular gobbled up local broadcast stations and conformed news reporting to their centralized point of view.[20] In 1996 the first corporate mainstream media was created for political purposes, called Fox News. Their coverage of political platforms and actions departed from portraying all politicians as self-motivated to selectively portraying one party as being better for America. The mainstream credibility of Fox News legitimized fringe media with the same political agenda.

---

[17] *The Scheme1: The Powell Memo*. (2021, May27). Senator Sheldon Whitehouse. From https://www.whitehouse.senate.gov/news/speeches/the-scheme-1-the-powell-memo/
[18] Whitehouse, S. (2021, May 17). *The Scheme 1: The Powell Memo*. Sheldon Whitehouse Speech Transcript. From https://www.whitehouse.senate.gov/news/speeches/the-scheme-1-the-powell-memo/
[19] Wikipedia contributors. (2025, Mar 4). *Fairness doctrine*. Wikipedia, The Free Encyclopedia. Retrieved 14:29, April 3, 2025, from https://en.wikipedia.org/w/index.php?title=Fairness_doctrine&oldid=1278793409
[20] Bauer, P. (2025, Jan 16). *Sinclair Broadcast Group*. Encyclopedia Britannica. From: https://www.britannica.com/topic/Sinclair-Broadcast-Group

The new millenia witnessed the rise in social media. Though this restored some diversity to "news" coverage, the dominance of our two party system meant that most of these "diverse" sources still conformed to two opposing party platforms, with even lower accountability than the news talk shows of broadcast media. Social media also took the emotional marketing of news to a new level for the sake of clicks and profit, engaging viewers with elevated anger, apprehension and entitlement. This emotional marketing for individual gain assaulted our brain and societal health.

We know now that since at least 2016 our social media has been invaded by other countries, mostly Russia and China, to sow division among citizens and distrust in government. While we have systemic flaws in governance to overcome, the distrust created by foreign governments has reached the extreme of people feeling violence is warranted for their political view to prevail.[21] Memes and other content are liked and shared without awareness that the trusted creator may be a bot with dubious intent. We also elected a President that claimed mainstream media was fake news … with the exception of the one mainstream media with a political agenda for supporting him.

During the 2024 election campaign, studies revealed that people who mainly get their news from social media (including YouTube) believe we are in a recession and unemployment is at a 50 year high. In reality, we had the fastest growing advanced economy in the world and unemployment was at a 50 year low at the time. In other words, a sizable portion of the country are being convinced figuratively that black is white, an Orwellian dystopia come true. The media devolved from creating cynicism at best to toxic emotions at worst, from providing investigative journalism to echo chambers of opinions, from the intimacy of local reporters to the remote authority of greedy influencers and foreign bots.

Of all the changes between "then and now," the changes to news media holds the most dire consequences for our collective wisdom.

Entry #6: Skepticism and Accountability

The country noted for introducing checks and balances to governance has an accountability problem. Unfortunately, many of our accountability problems cannot be remedied easily. The lack of term limits presents an accountability problem. The self-assigned judicial review power of the Supreme Court presents an accountability problem. The overlap in national, state and local jurisdictions presents accountability problems. The dearth of referendum voting at the national level, the conformity of a two party system and voter suppression laws make accountability problems difficult for the electorate to change.

---

[21] Wintemute, G., Robinson, S., Crawford, A., Tomsich, E., Reeping, P., Shev, A., Velasquez, B. & Tancredi, D. (2024, May 21). *Single-year change in views of democracy and society and support for political violence in the USA: findings from a 2023 nationally representative survey* . Inj Epidemiol 11(1):20. doi: 10.1186/s40621-024-00503-7. PMID: 38773542; PMCID: PMC11110245.

We cannot expect our leaders to fix accountability problems, since even a well intentioned leader seeks the efficiency of less accountability. Though the electorate recognizes the need to improve leadership accountability when calling for term limits, the zeal behind this call wanes for half the country whenever their own party controls Congress. We seem to believe that the solution to even longstanding problems like wealth disparity can only be fixed by keeping the right party in and the wrong party out in perpetuity, despite historical evidence to the contrary.

The growing wealth disparity since my youth relates to many of the trends that plague us. Many economic trends result from wealth disparity, such as increased poverty and spending cascades. Many political trends contribute to wealth disparity, such as the lack of accountability for our leaders. We fuel this in part by our tendency to blame only parties and politicians we distrust, while giving those we trust a free pass. To improve the accountability of both leaders and ourselves we must become skeptics.

Skeptics require a burden of proof for changing their minds, often along the lines of "seeing is believing." Distrusting a party, politician or news media to the extent that no burden of proof can change makes for a cynic, not a skeptic. Likewise, trusting a party, politician or news media to the extent that no benefit of the doubt can change makes for a zealot, certain in beliefs regardless of evidence.

Being certain about either what you trust or distrust closes you off from gathering further experiences, diverse news sources and greater wisdom. Sometimes this is warranted with well established facts; nobody attempts breathing underwater to gain additional experience or wisdom about our need for oxygen. However, the realms of policies, politicians and politics provide unlimited diversity for gaining wisdom from experiences if one chooses to be a skeptic.

When doing research I spend as much or more time examining the positions of those with whom I instinctively disagree. I either find a nugget of truth that previously escaped me, refining and changing my mind slightly, or bolster my knowledge about how alternative positions from mine fall short of the truth. This makes me a skeptic in search of wisdom. Just examining those I trust would instead conform me to their positions.

Election campaigns seek to conform rather than inform the electorate through pandering, thus nurturing groupthink over the collective wisdom that voting might achieve. The political base most capable of holding their own candidates accountable are also the segment of the electorate least likely to do so. Pandering through emotional appeals to fear, anger and entitlement erodes the brain health of a political base as well, making this a foundational concern for the *Unenlightened Wisdom Project*, with a mission of journeying from brain health to democracy.

Being skeptical need not oppose religious faith nor political trust. Religious faith depends in large part on things that cannot be "seen," and thus not subject to "seeing is believing." Political trust need not be abandoned simply because "seeing is believing" produces an occasional exception to that trust, instead skepticism requires a resistance to pandering even by those most trusted. Skepticism well practiced requires a humility towards one's own beliefs, even if strongly held, and keeping an open mind towards diverse experiences and news sources. By fulfilling this requirement, skepticism provides a gateway towards both wisdom, accountability and even brain health.

Yet how can skepticism prevail amidst the stress of mass society and complexities of political hierarchies?

Entry #7: Confronting Complexity and Conformity

A recirculating social media meme shows a horde of people turning left, guided by a sign for a pathway towards simple but wrong solutions. To the right heads a few people on a pathway towards complex but correct solutions. The meme implies that we need the best and the brightest to navigate us through the necessary complexities of civilization.

The meme misinforms people, since not all problems are complex, while some problems are made complex because of misinformation. Rather than having to depend on the best and brightest when misinformation makes a problem complex, a less authoritarian solution is to simplify the problem by removing the misinformation. For leaders who desire blind trust in their authority, misinformation and complexity become useful, empowering tools not to be acknowledged and remedied.

Long before the advent of social media, a cartoon showing a group of people flocking towards the simple but wrong solution would be labeled quite accurately as groupthink. After all, they are a group of people thinking the same way. Also of note, conforming people to the same way of thinking is the precise function of an interest group, particularly those known as political parties. Over time the use of groupthink has shifted to other terms changing the presumed locus of conformity.

Populism shifts the locus of conformity from a group to popularity among the masses. Yet obviously not all beliefs held in common by a mass of people results from conformity to beliefs, but rather from what we commonly experience. We each believe some popular things independently from each other, like going hungry is bad or reducing stress is good. When used disparagingly by pundits and politicians, populism implies conformity to beliefs that are not in a population's best interest. Ironically, buying into this authoritarian disparagement of populism is an example of groupthink.

Tribalism shifts the locus of conformity from a group to a tribe, failing to distinguish the difference between an interest group that coalesces around shared interests from tribes that historically coalesce around shared proximity. Though nomadic tribes conformed culturally in response to their shared living experiences, they had no concern for whether other tribes sharing different living experiences also conformed to the same set of beliefs in behaviors. In contrast, an interest group seeks to conform beliefs across all communities, all states, all living experiences. Ironically again, people buying into an academic misnomer of tribalism is groupthink.

To solve a problem we must first acknowledge we have one. Branding harmful conformity as populism acknowledges we need to solve the problem of the masses, or democracy. Branding harmful conformity as tribalism acknowledges we need to solve the problem of our primitive, tribal nature. Branding harmful conformity as groupthink acknowledges we need to solve the problem with blindly trusting interest groups to navigate complexity, including the interest groups known as political parties.

The previous entry called for us to become skeptics, requesting even the authorities we trust to satisfy a burden of proof for the sake of collective wisdom. Here is an equally important charge: Every time you hear populism or tribalism used by a politician or pundit substitute in your mind groupthink as the cause for harmful conformity in need of a remedy.

Entry #8: Free Market Misinformation

The previous entry reflected upon a social media meme that shows the masses heading in the direction of simple but wrong solutions. In reality, the masses often head in the direction of complex but wrong solutions, being herded by authorities that make something complex for the sake of gaining trust and power. Typically such authorities are the political parties that gain and conform our allegiance through misinformation.

The use of groupthink (which is neither populism nor tribalism if we are to respect the etymology of words), sometimes convinces society as a whole that black is white through obtuse and false assumptions. Both parties do this during election campaigns as they pander to the public. They often manipulate cherished ideals to gain support for policies not in the public's best interest. An example of this is pandering about freedom and related concepts such as free markets.

In the eighties conservatives frequently accused liberals of failing to understand the complexities of economics. The preceding decade of the seventies witnessed the dramatic increase of corporate funded think tanks that resulted from the 1971 Powell Memorandum to the US Chamber of Commerce (Entry #5). The memorandum essentially recommended the marketing (pandering?, campaigning?) of corporate ideology, with corporate funded think tanks acting as the marketeers. Liberals did not buy into this ideology and were accused of thinking with their hearts instead of their brains, thus labeled by such think tanks as "bleeding hearts."

Think tank pundits held that supply side economics best stimulated the economy. Policies that allowed for more wealth to be retained by corporations and the wealthy would trickle down to benefit the whole economy. Simple but sound logic suggests that concentrating wealth at the top of an economic system based on self-interest (greed) would not be shared in trickle down fashion. Ah, but think tanks claimed otherwise through their complex reasoning, and we are to believe that think tanks must be thinking great thoughts.

Nestled into think tanks thinking complex thoughts about supply side economics is the false assumption that government regulation of corporations infringes upon the free market ideal. Indeed, many think tank pundits refer to themselves as "free market libertarians," which contains the complexity of an oxymoron inside of an oxymoron. In reality, the conditions required for a shareholder corporation to exist are the antithesis to the requirements necessary for a free market to exist.

A market exchange requires the government coding, protection and enforcement of property value. Without those functions the exchanges would amount to bartering, where two sides negotiate the values of goods or services that can arbitrarily differ with each exchange. Nor could anything besides good faith protect the integrity of the exchange between two barterers. No rule making structure such as government means no markets.

Given that governments are responsible for markets to exist, the "free" in free market abides by a supply and demand model unaffected by coercion. The demand by consumers and supply by producers in creating a market must not be coerced or altered by either government or false information. Government coerces the market in favor of for profit corporations over proprietors, producers and consumers through decisions as blatantly oxymoronic and false as "corporations are persons,"[22] yet this government coercion alone is not sufficient for corporations that depend on continued growth to succeed. The marketing and/or lobbying they need to continually expand markets necessarily entails misinformation as well. Thus free markets and shareholder corporations are mutually exclusive. They never coexisted; if the meaning of concepts matter they cannot ever coexist.

In retrospect, economic data from the past few decades refutes trickle down economics. The decades of growing wealth disparity since the eighties correlates with trickle down policies, as do the related political causes of wealth disparity and economic consequences. The simple logic that concentrating wealth at the top will remain there when an economic system is driven by self-interest (greed) turns out to be more accurate than the complex, libertarian think tank justifications for supply side economics.

Meanwhile, society has been so indoctrinated into believing that corporations are an expression of free markets that politicians and pundits can use the misinformation as a red herring. Proponents of a shareholder driven economy use the false claim of free markets to justify for profit corporations, while critics of corporate abuses cite free markets as a cause of the problem. This leads to the brand of "dialectic reasoning" engaged in by political parties: proposed policy and counter policy "cures" over regulating what are essentially capital markets. Never exposed to the light of reasoning, dialectic or otherwise, is how to correct government from coercing favoritism towards shareholders over the other stakeholders of capitalism.

Historical data has shown "bleeding heart" liberals to be on the side of simple but correct logic in regards to trickle down policy, yet they should not feel too smug about this. Decades later they

---

[22] *Santa Clara County v. Southern Pacific Railroad Co.* 118 U.S. 394 (1886). U.S. Supreme Court.

now infuse political discourse with their own false assumptions about a cherished freedom ideal. Coming up next: claims of democracy.

Entry #9: Claims of Democracy

Enlightenment thinking produced three contrasting visions of human nature and their implications for governance. Thomas Hobbes viewed human nature as bad and we needed sovereign government to maintain an orderly society.[23] Citizens should obey their sovereigns under this view. John Locke viewed human nature as possessing foundational rights, yet advocated sacrificing some of those rights through a consent to be efficienty governed by representatives.[24] We could react to what was in our best interests, but were not competent enough to pursue such interests without the best and brightest representatives.

Jean Jacques Rousseau viewed human nature as essentially good, hence a democratic government should reflect the general will of the people.[25] Rather than citizens obeying sovereigns or trusting leaders, they should participate in their own governance. If we use Rousseau's perspective as our starting point, humanity had the character and competence to achieve collective wisdom; Locke thought our competence was flawed, at least for civilized governance, requiring representatives to govern on our behalf; Hobbes thought we were morally flawed, requiring authoritarian government to achieve civilized goals. Each type of government is logically consistent with its corresponding view of human nature.

Rousseau's vision has succeeded locally at town hall meetings, and at the level of state government through participatory referendums. Despite this success participatory government has not been practiced at our national level, with some pundits referring to Rousseau's vision of direct participation as extreme. Other rationales are used then to justify a more practical sort of democracy.

The peaceful transfer of power has been of concern lately as a defining characteristic of democracy. Yet many monarchies have a peaceful transition of power. Though they are necessary for maintaining order with any type of government, peaceful transitions are not sufficient for creating democracy. There must be more to the transitioning than simply being orderly.

---

[23] Hobbes, T. (2002). *Leviathan*. (A.P. Martinich, ed.). Broadview Literary Texts. (Original published 1651). From
https://books.google.com/books?id=YuBl1iaCw88C&pg=PR3&source=gbs_selected_pages&cad=1#v=o nepage&q&f=false
[24] Locke, J. (2025, Jan 15). *The Second Treatise of Government: An Essay Concerning the True Origin, Extent and End of Civil Government*. Wikisource. From
https://en.wikisource.org/wiki/Two_Treatises_of_Government_(unsourced)/Book_II
[25] Rousseau, J.J. (1998). *The Social Contract or Principles of Political Right*. (H.J. Tozer, Trans.) Wordsworth Classics of World Literature. (Original published 1762) From
https://books.google.com/books?id=YuBl1iaCw88C&pg=PR3&source=gbs_selected_pages&cad=1#v=o nepage&q&f=false

Pundits offer the liberty of free and fair elections as the added characteristic necessary for democratic transitions. The evidence of voter suppression and qualified citizenship refutes this claim for democracy on our behalf, but let us assume the mere intent for free and fair elections suffices. Intended free and fair elections effectively become fraudulent if elected representatives become corrupted when acquiring power, undermining liberty in the process. There needs to be some coded system to prevent subsequent corruption if one intends to have a democracy.

Our system of checks and balances between different branches of government has been our main claim as pioneers for democracy in a civilized world. Two branches are run by elected representatives, one by unelected and authoritarian judges. No participatory branch or function along the lines of Rousseau's vision was created to be checked and balanced along with these three. Void of this participatory element, representatives and authoritarians created the checks and balances to mitigate the corruption of representatives and authoritarians. What could possibly go wrong with that "democratic" system?

Peaceful transitions of power provide order; free and fair elections provide liberty; coded checks and balances mitigates corruption. We might desire all three rationales to be true for a democracy, but they also could be parts of other types of government. A claim of democracy should be rooted in the actual structures and function that define the concept, not simply because pundits or academics make such a claim.

Entry #10: What is democracy?

Ever since Trump first came into power Democrats have claimed him to be a threat to democracy. Both moderate Republicans and at least forty members of Trump's own former administration now make this claim as well, but the nature of party politics make Democrats the ones posting memes and YouTube videos claiming the stupidity of MAGA followers. The groupthink meme about people flocking to simple but wrong solutions has been circulated mainly by liberals, at least on my social media feeds. Such accusations reveal an ironic ignorance about our "democracy."

Researchers at Northwestern and Princeton analyzed policy decisions and concluded we do not have a democracy.[26] My earlier research of economic trends lasting decades concluded the same, with increasing wealth disparity serving as my shorthand reference to this research.[27] There are economic consequences to wealth disparity revealed by my research (as well as the research of others); there are legislative causes to wealth disparity that the Northwestern and Princeton researchers revealed. If wealth disparity does not strike a chord with you, consider the phrase "shrinking middle class." By no expected function for "democracy" would this type of growing trend occur for decades, which begs the question "What really is democracy?"

---

[26] Gilens, M. & Page, B. (2014, Sep. 18) *Testing Theories of American Politics: Elites, Interest Groups, and Average Citizens.* Cambridge University Press.
[27] Sinclair, K. (2009). *Systems out of Balance: How Misinformation Hurts the Middle Class.* Mill City Press.

Lincoln's famous quote in the Gettysburg address provided the widely accepted standard for the structure of a democracy: "government of the people, by the people and for the people." The "by the people" must be treated with a caveat. The complexities and hierarchies of mass society require at least some measure of representation to govern, similar to how a "free market" requires at least some involvement of government to maintain markets (Entry #8).

To be "of the people" the laws of a democracy need to apply equally to all. *The Unenlightened Wisdom Project* provides a comprehensive discussion about the structure of American governance failing this requirement; for current brevity consider exemptions from the law such as qualified and absolute immunity, or whether the punishments for white collar versus blue collar crimes are commensurate to the respective harms done. In regards to "for the people," consider five decades of growing wealth disparity and all the consequences "against the people" that entails. We fail at Lincoln's structural requirements for a democracy.

The function of any type of government should be wise rule. Hobbes envisioned the wise rule of strong authoritarians maintaining order; Locke envisioned the wise rule of the best and brightest representatives maintaining our foundational rights; Rousseau envisioned wise rule by direct participation (Entry #9). In essence, Rousseau envisioned the function of government to be collective wisdom. His belief in governance by the general will of the people also comes closest to Lincoln's structural definition of democracy being "by the people."

Some academics and corporate funded think tanks refer to Rousseau's vision of the social contract as extreme, inevitably leading to the decline of empires by indulged citizens. A fair question for these thinkers is whether Lincoln's structure and Rousseau's function for democracy ever existed for declining empires. In any case, such thinking fails to distinguish between groupthink and collective wisdom, two polar opposite conditions.

Collective wisdom is thwarted by our current two party system, no matter how smart or "stupid" the electorate. The parties coerce our choices for representatives through varied means ranging from gerrymandering to campaign financing to the disproportionate influence of incumbency. Political parties, politicians and pundits often misinform through pandering and propaganda. Our lack of skepticism for the authorities we trust, coupled with the groupthink they create, allows this misinformation to thrive and influence our choices. We do not satisfy the conditions of an informed and unimpeded electorate necessary for collective wisdom, participatory governance or Rousseau's and Lincoln's vision of democracy.

You cannot alleviate the threats to something that does not exist. Whereas Republicans and Libertarians of the eighties wanted to alleviate the threats to pretend "free markets," Democrats currently are the party most concerned about alleviating the threats to a pretend "democracy." Just as we should replace populism or tribalism with the more accurate description of groupthink, just as free markets should be replaced by the more accurate description of corporate markets, references to our "democracy" should be replaced by the more accurate "status quo" whenever encountered.

If you are exhorted to take pride in our democracy, consider that you really are expected to take pride in our political and economic status quo. If you are warned about threats to our democracy, consider that you are being warned against threats to our status quo instead. These are first steps towards eschewing groupthink for the democratic function of collective wisdom.

Entry #11: False Republic

We consider ourselves to be a constitutional republic. A republic, because we solve the "by the people" problem of mass society by voting for representatives to govern for us. Constitutional, because the Constitution sets the rules for how representatives will make laws on our behalf. The Legislative Branch makes laws; the Executive Branch executes them; and the Judicial Branch adjudicates how laws are executed.

We cite the Constitution for being a pioneering document for achieving democracy through a republic. The Founders even included a republican styled provision for amending the Constitution should flaws be discovered while we grew and learned as a country. Unfortunately, the Founders did not anticipate, nor has the amendment process rectified, a couple of governing flaws that prevent us from being a constitutional republic.

You will not find any mention of political parties in the Constitution, a reflection of the concern the Founders had for the divisiveness and partisanship that result from party biases. Here is what half of our Mount Rushmore of Presidents, and two out of the first three to hold that office, had to say about parties near the start of our nation's government:

"Let me now take a more comprehensive view, and warn you in the most solemn manner against the baneful effects of the spirit of party generally." - George Washington, Farewell Address, September 19, 1796

"If I could not go to heaven but with a party, I would not go at all." - Thomas Jefferson, Letter to Francis Hopkinson, March 13, 1789

Influenced by such distaste for political parties, the Constitution established checks and balances between branches of government, intended in part to avoid the partisanship of party politics. Unintended political parties still formed early on, but could go extinct if they became too unpopular. This happened first to the Federalist Party early in the nineteenth century, in large part due to an overreach of government with their Alien and Sedition Acts of 1798. Before John Adams left office he managed to pack the Supreme Court in 1800 with Federalists, believers in the type of government that led to their party being the first to go extinct. In the 1803 case of Marbury v Madison the Federalist packed court then gave themselves the authority of judicial review to determine laws as unconstitutional.[28]

---

[28] *Marbury v. Madison*. 5 U.S. 137 (1803). U.S. Supreme Court.

In the rules for making rules, the Constitution allowed the President to veto laws made by Congress, one of the checks between branches. However, Congress could then override a veto with a larger majority, still allowing the most representative branch of government to be the ultimate legislator of laws that the Constitution intended. The Constitution did not specify the role of judicial review for the Supreme Court, or indicate in any wording that unelected justices should determine which laws needed adjudication.

We are not a constitutional republic, outside of claiming we are, because of the unforeseen and unintended roles of political parties and the authority of the unchecked, unelected Supreme Court. Not a republic, because the supreme authority for the laws shaping our social systems are not elected representatives. Not constitutional, because political jurisprudence shapes the most important laws for our governance, not the Constitution.

In less than a week during the 2024 campaign, events highlighted the problems that result from the unintended power bestowed upon political parties and the Supreme Court. The early Presidential debate revealed one candidate in cognitive decline while the other disregarded truth and substance. Neither candidate represents the "best and the brightest" that representative government is supposed to offer in theory; they are the result of the party power and groupthink embedded in our political process.

The Supreme Court concluded its legislative, excuse me, judicial session shortly after the debate. One decision gave the Judicial Branch oversight authority over the decisions of Executive Branch agencies.[29] The only unelected, unrepresentative branch of government assumed executive authority to go along with its existing legislative authority.

Many countries patterned their representative government after ours, with a few caveats. Most advanced countries with the happiest and healthiest citizens do not assign judicial review to their high courts. Most do not have a two party system. None allows, as did our Supreme Court, campaign financing based on the principle that "money is free speech," or considered corporations as persons. Countries closer to reaching the ideals of democracy and republic learned from and chose not to adopt the mistakes we continue to make.

Many other countries considered to be democratic also have national referendums. Missing from our system of checks and balances is a participatory branch, say the Referendum Branch, to balance the representative and authoritarian branches. The function of such a branch would be determining accountability checks for other branches and political parties, as well as responsibility checks for shareholder corporations who owe their existence and competitive advantages to government. Checks on the participatory branch would be to prevent interest groups, news media and/or authoritarian driven groupthink to corrupt the collective wisdom of the electorate.

---

[29] *Loper Bright Enterprises v. Raimondo.* 603 U.S. 369 (2024). U.S. Supreme Court.

Of course, the problem with authoritarians and representatives being checked and balanced by a participatory branch is they are in charge of protecting or changing the system. They are more likely to dismiss accountability ideas as populist … and be accurate with that terminology.

Entry #12: Complex Federation

We are a democracy and republic because we say we are, but we neither have the structure nor function of either. We truly are structured as a federation, satisfying the criterion of a central government for a group of states that retains some autonomy for governing their own affairs. The original division that formed our political parties was over the balance between strong central government versus states rights, not conservatism versus liberalism.

Early on, a large majority of Americans favored states rights, unsurprising given the varied origins of different colonies. The Founders first created the Articles of Confederation to form a republic that reflected that majority preference, but the Articles did not provide our fledgling federation the authority needed to thrive amongst the other nations of the world. We created the Constitution to replace the shortcomings of the Articles.

The first major party to both come into power and go extinct, the Federalists, favored strong central government. The second major party favoring strong central government, the Whigs, also went extinct. The third time proved to be the charm when a party favoring a strong central government, known as Republicans, coalesced to preserve the Union. The opposing party that originally supported states rights, once known as the Democratic-Republicans, divided into two branches. The surviving branch still favored states rights at the time and became the Democratic party. The actions of both parties now favor a strong central government, regardless of what their pandering may claim, with ideological divisions forming more along conservative versus liberal lines.

For perspective on the functioning of federations, consider the UNITED states in comparison with the former Soviet UNION and the current European UNION. Our states are similar in population to the countries of both those unions. The members of the European Union favor the "states rights" approach of member countries retaining much of their autonomy, similar to our early colonies. The Soviet Union imposed a strong central government, the type of government inclined towards justifying any means to preserve the Union.

This perspective raises the question of what should be the purpose of federated governance. One potential purpose would be to partition what centralized and localized governments each do best. As the Founders soon discovered, centralized government works best with our international standing and global commerce. To the extent that some rights are natural or universal, centralized protection of those rights also makes sense.

Yet centralized power correlates with and typically causes a concentration of wealth that disadvantages local businesses and communities. During my numerous journeys on foot across

America, I observed and reported on what communities do for their own. I noted that pressing issues such as hunger and homelessness are resolved only at local levels. Some communities even refuse help from federal coffers in order to better resolve community needs their own way, a testimony to what localized autonomy can do for the straightforward issues that most affect our lives.

A federated system that clearly delineated different levels of governance could decentralize power for the resources that experientially impact our lives, but the complexity of our political system includes the overlap of functions between different levels of governance. Complexity forms a positive feedback loop, creating dependence on authorities and representatives who benefit from that complexity. At worst complexity becomes a tool for corruption, maintaining a marriage between centralized power and concentrated wealth. Consider the tax code and appropriation bills.

The unchecked supremacy of the Supreme Court contributes to our complex federation by deciding which rights states should have according to party ideology, rather than applying consistent principles of federation or law. The Supreme Court cannot be changed directly by elections, but the corruption of federation, republic and democracy by this authoritarian branch of government lie at the heart of most recurring campaign issues.

Entry #13: Contextual Recap

Election campaigns seldom provide enough context for sufficiently understanding an issue. Providing context thwarts the objectives of spin or pandering to create groupthink and win an election. Even when candidates feel secure they align with the electorate on any particular issue they may still spin it for maximum effect, since elections are about voting for the candidate rather than any single issue. The entries of this journal up until now served as contextual background for prominent campaign issues, with an an advocacy for skepticism, accountability and wisdom.

Previous entries detailed how the country changed politically, economically and culturally from when two forty somethings were our Presidential candidates in 1960. As a comprehensive indicator for these changes I referred to growing wealth disparity over decades, reflecting both the political causes and economic consequences of that disparity. The media creates an expectation for the electorate to be indulged by the politicians they support, while becoming more centralized and opinion based as a news source over the years.

Our conformity to political parties and ideology has grown as a result of these historical changes, reducing accountability and wisdom in our governance. The electorate becomes chided for flocking towards "simple but wrong" solutions when in reality they are being herded. Wrong solutions also tend to be artificially complex, such as by conceptual misinformation and misunderstanding.

Political and academic pundits use "populism" or "tribalism" instead of the more accurate "groupthink" in reference to being herded towards a bad idea, as well as pejoratively connoting a good idea that threatens the status quo. They use "free markets" in reference to corporate markets, obscuring the real meaning of both "free" and "markets" for economic exchanges. They refer to our political system as "democratic" and/or a "republic," despite falling short on the aspirational structures and function of either.

One more added context to consider is how social systems behave in similar ways to natural systems. Keeping either type of system in balance depends on feedback, environmental feedback for a natural system, information for a social one. The organisms in both types of systems select for traits that help them survive and against traits that do not, thus policies entrenching representatives and authoritarians is actually a feature of the system and not necessarily conspiratorial.

Representatives and authoritarians may select for economic and political solutions to issues with the best of intentions, but ultimately will reinforce representative and authoritarian governance at the expense of participatory democracy and collective wisdom. An issue that might be resolved otherwise through participatory government will continually provide fodder for an election campaign. A dive into these issues exposes flaws in our political and economic systems as well.

PART TWO: Campaign Issues

Entry #14: Abortion and the Social Contract

Entry #9 covered the three basic types of social contract between leaders and citizens which derive from a society's view of human nature. Thomas Hobbes advocated sovereignty based upon a dim view of humanity. John Locke advocated representative government that protected liberties and guided us. Jean Jacques Rousseau advocated for the will of the people through participatory government, based upon a positive view of humanity when uncorrupted by civilized influences.

Ever since the Supreme Court overturned Roe v Wade, we have witnessed all three visions of the social contract play out. Apart from the moral and practical considerations of abortion, the issue provides a foundation for which vision of the social contract you favor and support. That in turn may guide your position on issues that extend beyond abortion.

The overturning of Roe v Wade meant reproductive rights were to be granted or denied by the states. Some state legislatures maintained existing rights; some legislatures passed anti abortion legislation and some states held referendums. Red state referendums passed in favor of protecting at least some reproductive rights where Republican legislatures were otherwise opposed, confirming the national polling that a wide majority of the public favors these rights.

Neither party platform champions the state referendums manifesting Rousseau's vision of true democracy through direct participation, nor do they suggest that such participatory referendums be conducted at a national level. Indeed, the closest thing we have to something resembling a national referendum process is the Amendment provisions in the Constitution, which is actually a convoluted mixture of both representative and participatory governance. To participate directly and purely in decisions affecting your life you can do so only through state and local referendums.

Republicans of the MAGA movement agree with the overturning of Roe v Wade in favor of red state legislatures restricting reproductive rights, though some also favor Congressional action to restrict abortion rights at the national level. Considering that the Republican Party often runs on a platform of government being a problem, with decentralization the answer, state governments imposing laws against the known will of the majority exposes the hypocrisy of their position. In reality, the Hobbesian vision of authoritarian rule against the wishes of the flawed majority makes sense for a "law and order" party, at least in regards to reproductive rights.

When protesting Roe v Wade turning reproductive rights decisions to the states, Democrats reflect the Lockian vision for representative government legislating on our behalf. At least in regards to the reproductive rights referendums, Rousseau's democratic vision for participatory government achieves the same goal for states as would representative government. While either a representative or authoritarian government must exist in complex mass societies, why would Democrats not aggressively champion participatory referendums at the state level for straightforward, experiential issues such as reproductive rights?

Participatory government overcomes obstacles to the democracy Democrats claim we have, but representative government maintains the status quo that we truly have. Both would produce the same results for reproductive rights, but falsely calling the status quo a democracy matters when the results of government create deep dissatisfaction. The economic and health consequences of wealth disparity have increased for decades, no matter which party has represented us in which branch. Falsely equating the status quo with democracy therefore indicts direct participation by association, making an alternative authoritarian approach that manages the flawed majority an increasingly attractive solution.

This contrast of social contract visions left out moral and practical considerations for the reproductive rights issue. For some, moral intentions call for authoritarian rule over participatory referendums, while others see protecting reproductive rights as the moral thing to do. The next entry contrasts moral intentions with outcomes on abortion.

Entry #15: Abortion and Morality

Abortion bans against the will of the people adhere to the authoritarian view of humanity and the social contract: sovereign government and laws exist to maintain order because humans are morally irresponsible. The *Unenlightened Wisdom Project* counters that human physiology confirms that morally responsible behaviors enhance brain health. Authoritarian government that contradicts the intent of the majority therefore should be considered justifiable only if achieving an outcome not possible through direct participation that exercises moral responsibility. In the case of a government enforced abortion ban that outcome presumedly would be to reduce abortions, but the historical data from the Guttmacher Institute does not justify restricting reproductive rights on this basis.

Note from the data that abortion rates first went up after Roe v Wade in 1973. Contributing to this rise were legalized abortions becoming reported abortions done by clinics, as opposed to those previously done illegally and unreported. After that initial increase abortion rates steadily declined for decades to a rate lower than before Roe v Wade, as responsible family planning such as birth control became more effective. Note as well the correlation between the steepness in decline for abortion rates and the administration in office.

Family planning and government bans are separate strategies which might coexist in theory. Willing individuals can reduce abortions through family planning while authoritarian governments can reduce abortions through laws that force the unwilling. However, world data does not support this assumption.[30] A glance at the geography of abortion rates reveals that the lowest

---

[30] *Abortion Rates by Country* (2025). World Population Review. From
https://worldpopulationreview.com/country-rankings/abortion-rates-by-country

rates mainly come from European countries that protect reproductive rights, while underdeveloped countries with authoritarian governments tend to have higher abortion rates.

Number of abortions per 1,000 women aged 15-44 years, 1973-2020
data collected by the Guttmacher Institute

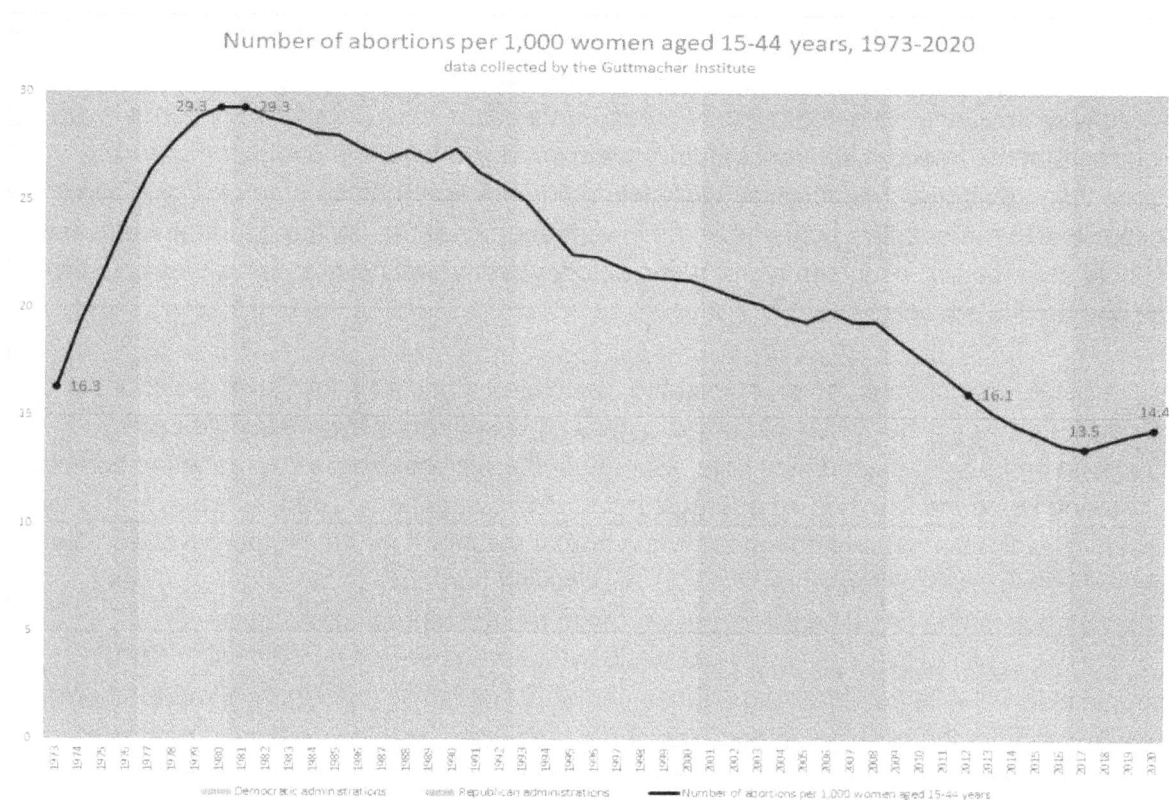

Correlation does not prove causation. A government ban on abortion does not directly cause abortion rates to increase, unless we assume people risk being punished for having an abortion out of defiance or spite. We must dig deeper to uncover the wisdom behind why protecting reproductive rights leads to fewer abortions.

Entry #16: Abortion and Collective Wisdom

The *Unenlightened Wisdom Project* defines the practice of wisdom as a practicality. Free and fair referendums are practical if they reflect the collective wisdom of the electorate. Yet neither party ever suggests legislation or platforms to hold national referendums, nor do political pundits. This warrants a closer look at the anatomy of collective wisdom behind the referendums for reproductive rights to understand why electorates should want them, and why our parties do not.

Personally, we gain wisdom through age with the accumulation of diverse experiences. From the diversity of our experiences we filter out what is most relevant to our journey in life. However, when experiences are limited they produce bias instead of wisdom. Considering that none of us can have infinite experiences, we all retain bias to some extent. The function of collective wisdom then is to aggregate more diverse experiences than individually possible, in order to normalize the diverse biases.

People in red states consistently voting to protect reproductive rights after the overturning of Roe v Wade suggests that participatory government for simple, straightforward issues actually produces wise solutions, as determined by measurable outcomes. Data for our country over time shows that the freedom inherent in family planning has a bigger impact upon reducing abortions than government restrictions, while world data reveals that the countries who allow the most choice with reproductive rights have the lowest abortion rates. Without further examination this should be a rousing endorsement of participatory government, with a win-win for both pro choice and pro life advocates.

When an issue is simple enough to understand, people will draw from their own experiences to make decisions. The wide variety of human nature and experience means a wide variety of perspectives and biases behind their vote. Some people will vote from the experience and bias from knowing someone who had an abortion that could have been avoided, or having successfully avoided abortion through providing humane support for the mother involved. Some people will vote from the experience and bias of believing humanity to be immoral. These experiences bolster the pro life call for legislatures to restrict reproductive rights.

Yet people also will vote from their experience and bias that family planning worked for them. Some will vote from the experience and bias of a tragedy that resulted from a woman being deprived of choice. Some will vote from the experience and bias of thinking that providing resources for children reflects greater morality than government restrictions. Even if unaware of the win-win results from protecting reproductive rights, supporters of pro choice may have an intuition that this leads to a more humane society overall.

World data supports the humane intuition from referendums normalizing the biases of diverse experiences. Authoritarian governments tend to impose restrictions on many things besides abortion, often targeting women. Authoritarian governments that override the responsibility and will of the people tend to have inferior education, health and happiness outcomes in comparison to those that attempt to enable that responsibility and will.

The argument for participatory government would be that aggregating and normalizing the biases of the many provides the collective wisdom that should be the function of a democracy, for even the "best and brightest" have biases. The Flip and Shift of our parties during my lifetime (Entry #2), reveals how fickle the biases of our representatives can be. Yet despite the win-win moral outcomes of red state voting for pro choice, the mainstream supporters of the political status quo will never call for more participatory government at either the state or national level. Their antidote for authoritarian state legislatures always will be the hope for a representative Congress to take charge. Any movement towards the collective wisdom from direct participation will be done by grassroots initiatives that buck party groupthink.

Entry #17: Healthcare Coverage and Costs

The moral outcomes of reproductive rights referendums provide an example for how collective wisdom can prevail through direct participation on an issue. When voting for representatives instead we hope they wisely decide for us, but other factors influence them in addition to their constituents. Interest groups provide lobbying to influence representatives and pundits to influence the public. In regards to healthcare, interest groups known as think tanks provide the lobbying and punditry to reduce the coverage and increase the costs of healthcare.

For decades our country had three growing healthcare problems. Many lacked coverage; healthcare costs more than doubled the average of other healthy countries;[31] and our life expectancy relative to other countries has decreased steadily over time (Introduction). The Affordable Health Care Act, or Obamacare, addressed only the first problem, yet Democrats tout AHCA as a crowning achievement for reforming a healthcare system that still depends on for profit corporations to insure the majority.

Presidents from Frankline Roosevelt to Lyndon Johnson supported some form of federal assistance with health insurance, but the American Medical Association stood in their way.[32] With little relevant context for objecting to this powerful interest group, for profit corporations continued to provide the main coverage for healthcare. Since then evidence accumulated confirming the cost savings for advanced countries with universal healthcare, but this global context contributes to our collective wisdom only if we are properly informed. Enter the corporate funded think tank!

Think tanks expanded dramatically since 1971 (Entry #8), with many of them having a healthcare mission. Their lobbyists influence the decisions of representatives and authoritarians, who are much easier to persuade than an electorate voting according to their healthcare experiences. On news media, think tank pundits brand healthcare policies supported by candidates like Bernie Sanders as radical, despite being similar to Eisenhower's economic philosophy (Entry #2).

To even get AHCA passed the same party had to control all of the House, Senate and Presidency. When Republicans similarly controlled all branches of government in 2016 they promised a plan that would be better than the AHCA. However, their plan had a flaw hugely unpopular even with their constituents, removing the protections for coverage of preexisting conditions. Republican leaders went so far as to accuse their own constituents of being "childish" if they objected to their flawed plan for replacing the AHCA.[33] The insufficient AHCA still remains in effect. The opposition even from conservatives to overturning the AHCA might

[31] *How Does the U.S. Healthcare System Compare to Other Countries?* (2024, August). Peter G. Peterson Foundation. From https://www.pgpf.org/article/how-does-the-us-healthcare-system-compare-to-other-countries/
[32] The Miller Center. (2025). *Presidents on health care*. University of Virginia. From https://millercenter.org/health-care-policy/presidents-health-care
[33] Last Week Tonight Library, S4 E5 (2017, Mar 12). *American Health Care Act*. YouTube. From: https://www.youtube.com/watch?v=qHKu1zMriyc

be considered an example of collective wisdom prevailing over think tanks, except that the other two problems of exorbitant costs and life expectancy still remain.

State referendums on healthcare are infrequent and likewise focused more on the extent of coverage than on total costs.[34] We are now even less likely to fix the most striking problem of costs than before, with more of the population now invested in the corporate driven system for profit. Think tanks, particularly those that ironically call themselves "free market libertarians," will continue their lobbying and punditry to maintain our for profit healthcare system. Of course there will be no national referendums on the matter, but why do state referendums on our grievously flawed healthcare system seldom occur, and then only push back on the coverage issue?

Entry #18: Health Insurance Boondoggle

For a few years after becoming a full time caregiver I chose not to have health insurance, as I had discovered that the cost of my family health insurance for three years as a high school teacher exceeded all my subsequent healthcare costs since then, without adjusting for inflation! Indeed, my last annual check up that I paid out of pocket was less than one third the cost of one month's family insurance 35 years ago. Had I foregone all insurance and paid my medical costs directly for thirty years I would have saved roughly the value of my house. Talk about for profit corporate boondoggles!

My greatest expense during those thirty years was surgery to repair a bunion. Most people obtain health insurance to prepare for much worse case scenarios than I suffered throughout my life. A relative of mine experienced such a scenario when he ended up in the hospital for 62 days due to complications from an aneurysm. To this day he continues to wear leg sleeves to manage his blood flow problems.

My relative is the rare exception where he would have come out financially better from having health insurance. As a small business owner my relative could not afford health insurance when the tragedy occurred and had to make financial arrangements to pay down his hospital debts over time. Both the hospital, which was not for profit, and his community helped out with this repayment. Now at age 88, his brain health allows him to still sing in a choir and live with his significant other. This worst case scenario did not end in the catastrophe people fear of landing in the figurative poor house, or even a literal nursing home. My relative continues to live beyond the life expectancy age for this or any other country.

Variety is the spice of life. Collective wisdom, as opposed to groupthink, requires diversity rather than conformity. The combination of nature and nurture will lead some people to live according to probabilities, others to prepare for worst case scenarios. Yet people in a society where worst case apprehensions meet up with the boondoggle of for profit insurance will have more debt and

---

[34] *Health Insurance Ballot Measures* (2018-2023). Open Secrets. From
https://www.opensecrets.org/ballot-measures/issues/health-insurance/21/2018

chronic stress than a society without for profit insurance. With chronic stress a leading cause for a wide variety of health problems, stress inducing healthcare costs that double those of any other country creates a positive feedback loop that benefits for profit insurers.

During a 5,000 mile walk across the country I encountered "Utah Matt," a man deeply dissatisfied with the corporation that recently laid him off. I suggested he work for a small business or start his own but he countered you have to work for a corporation to get decent pay … and the insurance package. Two states later I encountered "Kansas Matt," who was similarly fed up with corporate America in Denver and moved back to his small hometown. He combined five different endeavors into one synergistic enterprise to earn a living on his terms.

My tale of two Matts puts an ironic twist to the "free market libertarian" pundits and lobbyists who are funded well to advocate for the boondoggle of for profit insurance. For profit corporations cannot exist by free market principles no matter what they provide, while insurance does not abide by free market principles no matter who is the provider. Substituting the full value of wages with a partial diversion to expensive but speculative insurance restricts autonomy in seeking employment, not to mention what to do with the full market value of one's wages. Insurance packages also provide corporations a competitive advantage over proprietors for acquiring and retaining employees such as Utah Matt.

For profit corporations are aided further by government structuring the complex tax code to exempt insurance packages from the payroll tax. No "free market libertarian" think tank will ever cite the various costs to taxpayers and patients with this boondoggle. No "free market libertarian" lobbyist will ever point out how the government coerces markets to favor for profit corporations over proprietors with this boondoggle. No "free market libertarian" pundit will ever confess to news media outlets the constraints of liberty upon employees with this boondoggle. "Free market libertarians" that work for corporate funded think tanks serve their for profit corporate sugar daddies; not small businesses, not employees, not taxpayers or patients.

Which of the two Matts do you think was freer? Happier? Healthier? Kansas Matt, of course, for he embraced his autonomy in a society where interest groups seek to control our emotions and influence (market) what we think we can or should do. Health insurance is not the worst example of this. For that we turn to gun violence.

Entry #19: Fear and Gun Violence

When giving talks about my long distance journeys I am frequently asked what I do about bears. My standard reply is that if you know what you are doing, don't carry a salami in your pocket, etc, black bears in the wilderness are not the problem that bears who frequent campgrounds pose. At one particular talk an attendee interjected, before I could answer, that you need to carry a gun. Even after I explained that was not the case, he adamantly insisted that carrying a gun was the necessary solution. It did not matter that I was the experienced expert in the matter, he already had been convinced otherwise.

Related to this, an acquaintance posted on her Facebook profile the manner in which she dealt with a sketchy situation after returning from a day hike. From a hidden vantage point she observed a stranger still hanging around the trailhead who had been there when she left. Instead of proceeding to her car she remained out of sight and sent a text for a friend to meet her. When the friend arrived she continued on to her car and left the scene without further incident.

Most comments on the post consisted of relief and well wishes. However, one response called for owning and carrying a gun wherever you go, even though the anecdote demonstrated a solution that did not require one. Ironically, introducing a gun into this situation increases the likelihood that gun violence could have occurred, without a guarantee that the stranger had ill intent, or that the woman would be the first to pull the trigger. Carrying guns because of a needless fear of situations involving bears is one thing; a needless fear of situations involving humans is quite another.

The mantra "guns don't kill people; people kill people" suggests a solution to gun violence other than controlling guns. I agree with the mantra. Other high income countries, including those with high gun ownership rates, have far less deaths from guns per capita.[35] This then begs the question of what ultimately causes more people in our country using guns to kill people. Consider all the accidental gun deaths that occur in this country, particularly in states with "stand your ground" laws that encourage homeowners to shoot first and assess later. An extremely heartbreaking consequence of the shoot first mentality occurred with a Colorado man who shot and killed his stepdaughter after mistaking her for a burglar.[36]

A person who shoots first and assesses later feels threatened. A person who thinks guns are the answer for black bears in the wilderness feels threatened. A person who thinks an anecdote about avoiding danger without a gun proves the need to carry a gun feels threatened. Deranged mass murderers with assault rifles feel threatened. The popular mantra could be adjusted to warn: "guns don't kill people, people feeling threatened kill people." To address the ultimate cause for elevated gun violence in our country we need to understand why our society feels so threatened.

The answer does not lie in reality. For decades people have perceived that crime has increased each year.[37] In reality, violent crime has decreased.[38] The new adjusted mantra now becomes:

[35] Leach-Kemon, K., Sirull, R. & Glenn, S. (2023, Oct 31). *On gun violence, the United States is an outlier*. Institute for Health Metrics and Evaluation. From:
https://www.healthdata.org/news-events/insights-blog/acting-data/gun-violence-united-states-outlier
[36] KSDK Staff. (2013, Dec 24). *Colorado man kills stepdaughter after mistaking her for burglar*. KDSK 5OnYourSide. From:
https://www.ksdk.com/article/news/colorado-man-kills-stepdaughter-after-mistaking-her-for-burglar/308548122
[37] *U.S. crime rate - trend as perceived by the public 2024*. (2024, Nov). Statista. From:
https://www.statista.com/statistics/205525/public-perception-of-trend-in-crime-problem-in-the-usa/
[38] *Reported violent crime rate in the U.S. 2023*. (2024, Sep). Statista. From:
https://www.statista.com/statistics/191219/reported-violent-crime-rate-in-the-usa-since-1990/

"people feeling *falsely* threatened kill people." In the case of healthcare, hypothetical concerns are fed by a large host of "free market libertarian" think tanks, lobbyists and pundits. Gun violence provides an example of how just one, single interest group fuels falsely hypothetical fear and anger with their lobbyists and pundits. Any guesses for which interest group generates this toxic brand of groupthink?

Entry #20: The NRA Flip

The think tanks that blossomed in the seventies, many of them with a healthcare mission, served their corporate funders. The influence they have on our political and economic systems reflect the biases of their corporate sugar daddies. The NRA interest group was founded to serve members, thus representing the biases of that portion of the electorate. That turns out to not always be true.

Union officers founded the National Rifle Association (NRA) in 1871 to improve the atrocious marksmanship they observed during the Civil War. They also advocated responsible gun ownership and worked with government on gun restrictions during much of the twentieth century.[39] Assassination attempts using concealed weapons early on, the use of automatic weapons during the gangster era of the Roaring Twenties and the rise of gun violence during the upheaval of the sixties resulted in gun control measures backed by the NRA. With hunting being the most widely accepted and practical use of firearms throughout the twentieth century, gun owners had no apprehension that their guns would be taken away.

Alas, hunting has been in decline since 1960,[40] the unrest of the sixties lessened public acceptance of guns and the Gun Control Act of 1968, ironically backed by the NRA, threatened the profitability of gun sales. One hundred years after the NRA was founded, the Powell Memorandum of 1971 led to a boom of corporate funded interest groups with lobbyists (Entry #5). Some interest groups formed to promote specific causes, but gun manufacturers already had an existing one to influence. After the NRA created their lobbying arm in 1975, called the Institute for Legislative Action, they became the main instrument for gun manufacturers to reverse gun control legislation.[41]

With hunting in decline a new purpose for owning firearms needed to fuel the growth of gun manufacturing. NRA outreach focused on security in the face of mounting violent crime, even when such crime in fact was diminishing (Entry #19). They also framed gun control legislation as a slippery slope assault upon the entitlement of the Second Amendment. The interest group completely flipped their original mission of promoting gun responsibility to protecting gun rights

---

[39] Elving, R. (2017, Oct 10). *What is the NRA? A History, And 9 Facts You Might Not Have Known*. NPR. From: https://www.npr.org/2017/10/10/556578593/the-nra-wasnt-always-against-gun-restrictions

[40] *The Decline of Hunting and Fishing*. (2022). Wildlife for All. From: https://wildlifeforall.us/resources/decline-of-hunting-and-fishing/

[41] Elving, R. (2017, Oct 10). *What is the NRA? A History, And 9 Facts You Might Not Have Known*. NPR. From: https://www.npr.org/2017/10/10/556578593/the-nra-wasnt-always-against-gun-restrictions

as an entitlement, often against the wishes of overall society, and sometimes their own members.

The flip of the NRA provides a case study for how interest groups can impact the collective wisdom of a society. The neuroscience of brain health reveals that an autonomous person, socially engaged and relatively free from stress, wants to be responsible to others. An interest group of people with relevant experiences to a particular type of responsibility adds to the collective wisdom of a society. For its first hundred years gun owners became members of the NRA with a goal of responsibility. For one hundred years the NRA gained the trust of responsible members before herding them into demanding unchecked entitlement.

A majority of NRA members support background checks for gun ownership. This remnant nod to responsible ownership logically follows from the mantra of "people kill people." Yet the NRA successfully lobbies against even background checks, demonstrating their aversion to both responsibility and the wisdom they once contributed to society as a gun control advocate.

Gun owners have the most relevant experiences in regards to the responsibility of gun ownership, but society as a whole has abundantly relevant experiences with gun violence. Society as a whole overwhelmingly supports gun control measures to reduce violence. Because of their flipped mission to protect gun rights, ultimately for the sake of corporate gun manufacturers, the NRA herds members into groupthink that favors entitlement over responsibility.

The NRA marketing tools of fear, anger and entitlement also strike a blow against autonomy and brain health, a consequence of particular focus and concern for the *Unenlightened Wisdom Project*. Should such a study ever be done, I predict that NRA members have greater rates of dementia and lower life expectancy than the population as a whole, due to being bombarded with hypothetical and hyperbolic "slippery slope" and "dangerous society" arguments.

Entry # 21: Immigration Pandering

Participatory decision making through direct voting on reproductive rights (hence, true democracy) demonstrated humanity can achieve collective wisdom instead of groupthink when issues are uncomplicated and relevant to their experiences. Unfortunately, many issues are too complex for participatory government, while others hold only a remote relevance to our own lives. This enables the herding into groupthink called pandering, using similarly toxic means for brain health as used by interest group punditry. In such cases we may not be able to apply collective wisdom through participatory government, but might still apply skepticism towards pandering that leads us astray for both our brain and social health.

Different types of immigrants enter the country by different means, for different reasons, with different impacts on a country with varied opinions about immigration. The causes for immigration occur at multiple scales. Global economics and politics result in supplies of people leaving their countries. Our country creates a national demand for drugs and cheap labor. Some states have borders that can be crossed illegally in some states, putting pressure on that region's resources. The complex combination of causes, effects and scales of immigration provides an issue tailor made for pandering!

The United States as a global leader could play a key role in addressing the global causes behind mass immigration, but this issue calls for responsibility. Entitlement, not responsibility, is the currency of panderers. Remedying cheap labor might be good for laborers, but not for consumers and even less so for the investors. Considering that investors contribute the most money to the political pool of panderers, with consumers their targets, remedying cheap labor becomes a dead issue for immigration pandering.

Much of drug trafficking happens through legal ports of entry by people who are not immigrating. To make this issue suitable for immigration pandering, politicians stretch the truth to attach a national problem with legal ports of entry to the regional problem of illegal border crossings. If you are going to stretch the truth, why stop there? Undocumented immigrants become a criminal element, despite wanting to remain in the country unnoticed. They benefit from our taxpayer funded safety nets, despite not having a social security number required for securing them. They even eat our pets! These are tall tales that large segments of the electorate are unable to confirm or refute from personal experience.

Entitlement is about what people think they deserve, with a flip side of what is undeserved by others. Both sides of that coin work well for panderers, but the flip side of what people do not deserve provides a distraction, a target, an alternative villain for focusing the anger of an electorate disadvantaged by systemic problems that benefit the panderers. Which brings us to immigration pandering over a border wall.

Congress passed the Secure Fence Act in 2006 with the original intention of building 654 miles of wall along the most accessible areas of the southern border.[42] Both the Bush and Obama administrations built hundreds of miles, virtually achieving the original goal. Trump campaigned on extending the goal towards all 2,000 miles of the southern border, but had built only 52 miles of new wall by the end of his four years in office.[43] He claimed to have built 500 miles of new wall, but 95% of those miles consisted of repairing or reinforcing the already existing wall.

The border wall attempts to cure an immigration problem, but for motivated immigrants "where there is a will, there is a way." Many miles of wall needed to be repaired or reinforced because many miles of wall had been breached. The border wall neither reduces the large supply of motivated immigrants wanting to get in, nor curbs the domestic demand for bringing in cheap immigrant labor. With more miles of new wall being added, more miles will be breached. We

---

[42] Wikipedia contributors. (2025, January 23). *Secure Fence Act of 2006*. Wikipedia, The Free Encyclopedia. Retrieved 14:14, April 3, 2025, from https://en.wikipedia.org/w/index.php?title=Secure_Fence_Act_of_2006&oldid=1271220273

[43] Uribe, M. (2023, Aug 9). How many miles of border wall did Donald Trump build? Politifact. From: https://www.politifact.com/factchecks/2023/aug/09/donald-trump/how-many-miles-of-border-wall-did-donald-trump-bui/

still have over 1300 new miles to build on the southern border. More miles of new wall mean more miles of new repairs and reinforcements, which means a boondoggle of large maintenance costs in perpetuity.

With drug smuggling on the rise through the northern border, a solution to this regional problem affects us northern folks more than building a wall down south. Consider that we share 5,525 miles of border with Canada. If us northerners had to rely on state taxes and regional resources to build such an extensive and ineffective wall we would find another solution. I suspect the same to be true even for our shorter southern border, but regional issues only provide value for herding support if turned into a national concern.

A wall covering the entire southern border will never be finished as repairs, maintenance costs and ineffectiveness increase. That makes this issue ideal for political pandering, especially if voters can be convinced the cause is ineffective government. The border wall checks all the panderer's boxes:

> **P**erpetuated pandering of the issue
> **A**voids voter responsibility for a solution
> **N**ice boondoggle for benificiaries of the system
> **D**emonization of people instead of a system
> **E**lusive experiential verification of claims by voters
> **R**esists comprehension of an overall problem

Most pandering (and marketing) combines a few of these ingredients, but seldom do they all come together quite as well as with the proposed border wall. At least until the global causes of immigration are addressed, the border wall will be a campaign issue for many elections to come.

Entry #22: The Economy

We do not have a free market economy, nor even aspire to have one (Entry #8). Most governments influence markets directly through policies, and indirectly by being the only means through which a corporation for profit can exist. Our own government additionally tips the scales in favor of for profit corporations over proprietorships and other economic stakeholders through legislation and adjudication. Over the past few decades, "too big to fail" justifies bailouts and subsidies working in favor of the financial industry and shareholders, even as bankruptcy laws become tougher on small businesses and other stakeholders.

Should politicians ever focus on global causes of mass immigration, an understanding of the two basic economic philosophies that guide nations would contribute to our collective wisdom for the issue. Greatest average utility (GAU) seeks to maximize economic growth, building upon the philosophy of utilitarianism founded by the Enlightenment philosopher Jeremy Bentham.[44]

---

[44] Bentham, J. (1907). *An Introduction to the Principles of Morals and Legislation*. United Kingdom: Clarendon Press.

Bentham in turn was influenced by the Enlightenment philosophers John Locke and Thomas Hobbes,[45] whose social contracts advocated representative or authoritarian governments respectively to compensate for the shortcomings of humanity (Entry #9).

John Rawls was a post Enlightenment philosopher that founded the maximin principle of economics challenging GAU.[46] His own philosophy drew upon the works of Jean Jacques Rousseau and Immanuel Kant.[47] Rousseau was the social contract philosopher who had the most positive view of humanity and advocated participatory governance that aligns with true democracy (Entry #9). Kant asserted there are moral categorical imperatives that should be obeyed.[48] The maximin principle combines these two philosophies by asserting that policies should maximize the conditions of those worst off in an economy.

The global economy abides by the GAU economic philosophy. We maximize global economic growth with the economies of different countries focusing on what they do best. Focusing on natural resource extraction does not produce as much wealth as advanced technologies, leaving most countries at the bottom of the GAU ladder impoverished. GAU also justifies tipping the scales to favor for profit corporations and a business model that maximizes investment growth. Many economic think tanks use the slogan "a rising tide lifts all boats" as a catchy justification for why we should favor GAU policy.

High income countries benefit the most from a global GAU policy that concentrates wealth, power and influence, yet many of these countries apply a maximin principle to their own domestic economies. These countries tend to have less wealth disparity, greater life expectancy, better mental health and more happiness than countries with domestic economic policies that favor GAU and "rising tides." However, politicians and corporate funded think tanks refer to such maximin countries as socialist if they proactively limit the negative externalities created by for profit corporations, or welfare states if they reactively address these externalities.

Such think tank punditry and political pandering ignores the reality that, under free market conditions, for profit corporations could not compete or even exist. With free market conditions the concentration of wealth through earned income would be exponentially less than possible through investment growth, as would the negative externalities that maximin policies attempt to mitigate. Actual free market conditions also are much easier to understand than corporate markets masquerading as free markets, making them better suited for the collective wisdom of participatory governance.

---

[45] Driver, J. (2022). *The History of Utilitarianism*. The Stanford Encyclopedia of Philosophy (Winter 2022), E. Zalta & U. Nodelman (eds.). From
https://plato.stanford.edu/archives/win2022/entries/utilitarianism-history/.
[46] Rawls, J. (2009). *A Theory of Justice*. United Kingdom: Harvard University Press.
[47] Wenar, L. (2021). *John Rawls*. The Stanford Encyclopedia of Philosophy (Summer 2021), E. Zalta (ed.). From https://plato.stanford.edu/archives/sum2021/entries/rawls/.
[48] Johnson, R. & A. Cureton. (2024). *Kant's Moral Philosophy*. The Stanford Encyclopedia of Philosophy (Fall 2024), E. Zalta & U. Nodelman (eds.). From
https://plato.stanford.edu/archives/fall2024/entries/kant-moral/.

Just as actual free market conditions would limit wealth disparity within a nation, in theory it should accomplish the same objective globally. Limiting weatlh disparity globally means less impoverished nations and less corruption of their leaders. Less impoverished nations and corruption means less mass immigration and the problems that present. Unless we alter course towards real free market conditions, these problems will persist in perpetuity.

We would need to stop being swayed by punditry and pandering pretending free markets exist before becoming wise enough to address mass immigration and other problems caused by government coded and protected wealth disparity. This brings us to issues of fiscal and monetary policy.

Entry #23: Monetary Policy

Here is a conundrum. Which President or party did a better job of controlling inflation? At the end of 2019, the third year of Trump's term before the pandemic hit, our inflation was 2.3%.[49] Global inflation was at 3.5%.[50] At the end of 2023, the third year of Biden's term, our inflation was 3.4%, while global inflation was at 6.8%. Do we credit Trump for the lower inflation rate before an election year? Or do we credit Biden for better outperforming the global economy before an election year?

Fiscal policy, monetary policy, corporate policy, the global economy and unforeseen events impact inflation. The President can propose fiscal policies, but Congress has to be on board. The President can affect corporate policies, but ultimately only if the Supreme Court approves. In theory, the President does not dictate the monetary policies set by the Federal Reserve, but who knows what goes on behind closed doors. The same can be said for the global economy. The President of the United States may be the most influential person on earth, but does not have dictatorial control over many global inflationary factors.

Inflation involves "too much money chasing too few goods." High income countries have higher costs of living, as predicted by the "too much money" principle. As long as our country remains near the top of the global economic pyramid, created by an investment growth model predicated on GAU philosophy (Entry #22), our costs will be inflated relative to most other countries. We achieve higher standards of living by consuming foreign goods at less cost than what our domestic income from labor and investments would otherwise warrant.

"Too much money" concentrated at the top of the wealth pyramid leads to spending cascades for domestic products.*[51] Hefty levels of disposable income allows the wealthy to outbid and overpay for goods such as housing, which cascades down to overpaying for modest homes.

[49] *CPI and Inflation Rate for the United States*. (2019). CPI Inflation Calculator. Retrieved 2024 from https://cpiinflationcalculator.com/2019-cpi-and-inflation-rate-for-the-united-states/

[50] O'Neill, A. (2025, Jan 10). *Global inflation rate from 2000 to 2029*. Statista. Retrieved April 2025 from https://cpiinflationcalculator.com/2019-cpi-and-inflation-rate-for-the-united-states/

[51] Frank, R.H., Levine, A.S. & O. Dijk. (2014). *Expenditure Cascades*. Review of Behavioral Economics (Vol. 1: No. 1–2, pp 55-73). From http://dx.doi.org/10.1561/105.00000003

Whenever you hear "rising tides" used by think tanks to justify an investment growth model, be mindful that five decades of "spending cascades" applied to domestic goods such as housing, health care and education have drained your finances faster than the rising tides can lift them.

The flow of money impacts inflation more than the overall supply. Stimulus checks during the pandemic did not inflate costs because people were staying home and not spending. Tax cuts that disproportionately benefit the rich no longer inflate costs because so much wealth has been concentrated that the wealthy can convert much of their "disposable" income to some form of hidden, nontaxable or deferred taxable wealth. While such hidden wealth does not increase the flow of money, neither does it stimulate production or compensate the producers. Stimulus checks and tax cuts fall under the category of fiscal policy, but our focus for controlling inflation has been on monetary policy.

Both private and public debt increases the flow of money by providing immediate access to capital not otherwise available, with private debt exceeding public debt by almost 50%, $27 trillion to $19 trillion.[52] Monetary policy attempts to control the amount of debt with the Federal Reserve setting interest rates. When inflation is high, interest rates are raised to make borrowing costlier, thus curbing the flow of money. When inflation becomes low interest rates are lowered to encourage borrowing and stimulate the economy. .

Managing inflation through interest rates moderates the ebb and flow of money for the financial industry and investors, but exacerbates that ebb and flow for consumers and producers. Monetary policy could instead tighten the conditions for acquiring private debt, but this would require finding ways to help consumers without increasing the indebtedness that benefits investors and the financial industry. Such a strategy runs counter to the investment growth model that dictates economic policy.

Fiscal policy also holds the potential to cushion producers and consumers, but the extreme complexity of our tax code and appropriation bills puts fiscal policy out of reach for a society's collective wisdom. We must depend entirely on representatives or authoritarians to navigate the complexity of taxation and appropriation for us, and you seldom hear interest groups or politicians calling to make the system simpler. Let us therefore take a closer look at the absurd complexity of government revenues and spending.

Entry # 24: Taxation and Appropriation

There is a retired billionaire with a YouTube channel that analyzes government data, allegedly reporting on "just" facts and data without any bias. Assertive claims of being unbiased sends a warning signal, along the lines of "one doth protest too much," considering that even the most

---

[52] Vague, R. (2016). *The Private Debt Crisis*. Democracy Journal.(Fall 2016, no. 42). From https://democracyjournal.org/magazine/42/the-private-debt-crisis/#:~:text=One%20of%20the%20key%20 and,%5BSee%20Chart%202.%5D

fair minded people are biased by the experiences that shape their lives. When I watched a second video featuring taxes, his bias as a billionaire surfaced.

The billionaire showed data that the wealthy pay a disproportionate share of taxes. Of course they do! What he did not show was that the wealthy pay a lesser share of their wealth in taxes than middle class citizens.[53] The billionaire presented data giving the appearance that the rich pay more than their fair share when the opposite is true.

A coalescing theme for this election campaign series has been the growing wealth disparity for decades, regardless of which party controlled the Executive or Legislative Branch. Our system of taxation provides the foundation for this disparity, yet the tax code remains far too complex for the collective wisdom of even a well-informed society. This complexity requires authorities to fathom, which benefits representatives or authoritarians seeking our dependence upon their authority.

Government codes wealth into taxable, nontaxable and deferred taxation categories in ways that favor the wealthy and investors over other stakeholders of capitalism. We tax in a few different ways (property, sales, income, capital gains, payroll, tariffs), at different levels from local to federal. Corporations have the means to employ accountants and lawyers to navigate this labyrinth of taxes, while employing lobbyists to maintain such complexity. Just the federal tax code alone is 6,871 pages, with 75,000 pages of connected documents to entirely outline the system.[54]

The spending side of our fiscal policy features more excessive complexity. The federal budget includes both discretionary and mandatory spending. Taxes on income cover two items of mandatory spending, most other revenue forms a general fund to cover all other mandatory and discretionary items. The federal budget overlaps with state and local governments with items such as education, confusing both goals and funding.

Federal appropriation bills may seem diminutive compared to the tax code, generally in the neighborhood of 1,000 plus pages, but they sometimes include pork barrel projects and earmarks that benefit particular states rather than the nation as a whole. They also can contain "poison pills," legislation that has more to do with party ideology than spending. Political procedures and partisanship further complicate how bills get passed or merely voted on. This complexity of fiscal policy thwarts the collective wisdom of proprietors, laborers or consumers, despite being a tool that buffers inflation in a manner that benefits them rather than investors and the financial industry.

---

[53] Hanlon, S. & N. Buffie. (2021, Oct 7). *The Forbes 400 Pay Lower Tax Rates Than Many Ordinary Americans*. Center for American Progress. From
https://www.americanprogress.org/article/forbes-400-pay-lower-tax-rates-many-ordinary-americans/
[54] Consolidated Appropriations Act of 2024. HR 4366. 118th Congress (2023-2024). From
https://www.congress.gov/bill/118th-congress/house-bill/4366/text

We potentially could adjust pieces of fiscal policy if they were better understood and decided by national referendum, in keeping with true democracy. For our household budgets we understand the wisdom of taking on an extra job to acquire the funding for a specific goal. Our fiscal policy applies this approach with Medicare and Social Security, pairing up specific taxes on income with two mandatory spending items in our budget. If unfettered by groupthink we have the experiences necessary to apply collective wisdom towards such a budgetary approach.

Moving towards a wiser, more informed society would broaden this budgetary approach to items such as defense spending, by far the greatest discretionary expenditure. This means making defense spending mandatory (or else who are we kidding?) with specific taxes to cover that item. Taxes on capital gains, corporations, or tariffs would be the most appropriate target, since our military protects international commerce and the global application of the greatest average utility principle (GAU). Consider that trillions of dollars have disappeared into a sinkhole of unaccounted defense spending.[55] Targeting the revenue from the demographic mainly involved with those decisions will tighten up corrupt and unaccounted spending considerably, rather than allow the politics of defense spending to effectively "play with house money." An added bonus for brain heath would be reducing the fear and anger used as tactics to justify continued expansion of fiscal policty in this area.

For the collective wisdom of our society, the overlap between different levels of government for fiscal policy needs to be reduced and simplified. We do this to a certain extent with revenue, such as property taxes only being local and tariffs only being federal, but we could further simplify the level of our quite varied revenue streams. The same could be done with spending. Local governments are wiser with implementing basic needs policies, federal governments with international commerce.

For the collective wisdom of our society, appropriation bills need to be reduced and simplified. This would benefit even our selected representatives, very few of whom actually read a 1,000 page appropriation bill for themselves. Pork barrel projects and earmarks should be eliminated and put into the realm of greater state revenue streams and decision making as needed. The complicated procedural matters that fosters partisanship should be eliminated from the process.

Where we already could gain from the collective wisdom from our society is to put in the form of national referendums whether taxes should be paid in proportion to the wealth one holds. If we pair such referendums with appropriate data we could resist the political pandering and the complexity that has led some billionaires to pay nothing in taxes, while other billionaires create podcasts of "just" facts that do not actually relate to a principle of proportional wealth fairness.

I never got around to watching a third video from the "just the facts" billionaire.

---

[55] Gledhill, J. (2023, Dec 04). *Pentagon can't account for 63% of nearly $4 trillion in assets*. Responsible Statecraft. From https://responsiblestatecraft.org/pentagon-audit-2666415734/

Entry #25: News Media Systems

Entry #5 of this journal provided historical context for how two news media systems changed over the past sixty years. In summary, we have less local news media and investigative journalism, more mainstream news media and punditry. Two additional news media systems have become influential since then. Each system has a different bias and agenda from the others, creating different impacts upon the collective wisdom of our society.

– Local News Media Bias
Local news media reports on local events, biased by the culture, politics and economics of the local society. This is true "tribalism," though you are unlikely to ever hear a pundit use the term in this way, with each local "tribe" unconcerned about the news events and culture of other localities (Entry #7). Factual investigations benefit the local "tribe" more than punditry. Tribal diversity and investigative journalism benefits collective wisdom through a means used to aggregate and filter that diversity and factual journalism for national relevancy.

Research has linked the decrease in local news reporting to the increase of national divisiveness and partisanship.[56] As biased as any local tribe may be, theirs is a unique bias shaped by their independent set of experiences that do not conform to the biases of another local tribe. The conformity of various tribes to a common set of biases and beliefs must be induced externally by interest groups or authorities in the pursuit of groupthink. I plead with you again to substitute the term "groupthink" in your mind whenever you hear pundits talk about "tribalism" or "populism."

– Mainstream News Media Bias
Mainstream media is corporate owned, thus corporate biased. Global economics of greatest average utility (GAU) favors large corporations, thus mainstream news media inherently have this philosophical bias. Shareholder capitalism holds the reins of this global economy, explaining why stock market indicators are by far the most cited economic data on mainstream news media, much more than wealth disparity indicators. Corporate news media coverage also comfortably confuses the reality of capital markets with the ideal of free markets (Entry #8), creating a problem of identity similar to confusing "groupthink" with "tribalism."

The investment growth model driving for profit corporations and shareholder capitalism wants to continually expand markets, which means appealing to all demographics. When manifested in corporate mainstream media this gets labeled as culturally "woke" or "liberal" by conservative panderers and pundits, when in reality it is economically attending to the bottom line.

The status quo of government and the corporate biases of mainstream news media have a mutually beneficial relationship. Even so, the mission of most mainstream news media is still the news, not a political agenda. Mainstream news media readily retracts any reporting proven to be factually wrong. They may still get sued for a harmful story, but the lawsuit is not

---

[56] Darr, J.P. (2024, Jul 17). *Does local News Reduce Polarization?* Carnegie Reporter (Summer 2024). From https://www.carnegie.org/our-work/article/does-local-news-reduce-polarization/

necessary for the retraction of an investigative falsehood. This has become a critical distinction to make about this news media type in light of developments since the eighties.

– Fringe News Media Bias
Fringe news media bias favors alternatives to the status quo of party government, the global economy or the diversity championed by the mainstream. This can mean anything from progressivism to nationalism, with extremes ranging from anarchy to fascism. Fringe media has been filling the gap created by the shrinking of the local news media ecosystem, without substituting the service of factual, local reporting.

Unrelenting trends such as the causes and consequences of wealth disparity creates and fuels a demand for fringe media. However, the advent of social media enables anyone with a cam and enough followers to provide fringe news, with content ranging from insightful analysis of empirical data to wild conjecture and unchecked falsehoods, the latter not being "news" at all. The fringe also can be foreign actors with malicious intent for our governance, the farthest extreme possible from the tribal bias of local news media. This contributes to the increase in national divisiveness accompanying the shrinkage of local news reporting

– Bad Faith News Media Bias
Providing news under false pretenses has created a bad faith news media system.
Acting like wolves in sheep's clothing, pretending to be something they are not, characterizes this news media ecosystem. Sinclair Broadcasting Corporation (SBC) falls under this category by owning a large share of the local broadcast market for which they provide centralized content.[57] Fox News pretends to have a news media agenda, when in reality Australian business tycoon Rupert Murdoch and political operative Roger Ailes created Fox News to promote a Republican agenda.

With this media system, fringe news media feeds the SBC conglomerate and Fox News much like local news reporting used to feed the mainstream. Echo chambers form among fringe media sources, Fox News and "local" SBC stations. Since providing news is not the primary goal of SBC or Fox News, falsehoods from fringe media that serve their political agenda is prioritized.

Extending the sheep metaphor further, the bad faith news media convinces viewers they are privy to news not provided by the mainstream media herding their followers like sheep into accepting the status quo. (I believe the insult "sheeple" came from followers of this news media system.) Viewers are unaware of the occasions when their exclusive news is exclusively false, unaware they also are being herded into groupthink with propaganda.

The 2020 election revealed a third characteristic of the bad faith news media system, while also measuring the impact of groupthink. Unlike mainstream media, bad faith news does not retract proven falsehoods unless sued, and even then will settle out of court rather than have their

---

[57] Chang, A. (2018, Apr 6). *Sinclair stations map: Sinclair's takeover of local news, in one striking map*. Vox. From https://www.vox.com/2018/4/6/17202824/sinclair-tribune-map

fraudulent reporting revealed.[58] Trump challenged the 2020 election based on the wild conjecture and unchecked falsehoods that this news media system echoed. The January 6 committee televised their hearings during which members of Trump's own administration admitted he had known he lost the election legitimately, but the Fox News echo chamber did not provide hearing coverage.

This helps to explain why four years after the 2020 election, about one third of people polled still did not think Biden was the legitimate President.[59] Balancing out a one third voting bloc of conforming groupthink requires 75% of voters who have not been herded. This reveals bad faith news media to be a more formidable obstacle to collective wisdom than either punditry or pandering. Taking steps towards collective wisdom, participatory government and true democracy as a society requires neutralizing the impact of all three.

---

[58] Bauder, D., Chase, R. & G. Mulvhill. (2023, Apr 18). *Fox, Dominion reach $787.5M settlement over false election claims*. AP News. From https://apnews.com/article/fox-news-dominion-lawsuit-trial-trump-2020-0ac71f75acfacc52ea80b3e747fb0afe

[59] Fortinsky, S. (2024, Jan 02). *One-third of adults in new poll say Biden's election was illegitimate*. The Hill. From https://thehill.com/homenews/campaign/4384619-one-third-of-americans-say-biden-election-illegitimate/

PART THREE: Collective Wisdom

Entry #26: Perspective and Wisdom

To collect wisdom from an electorate, a society must first decide whether that is possible and desirable. Those with an authoritarian perspective on flawed humanity do not think collective wisdom from the masses is possible. Those with a "best and brightest" faith in leaders believe representatives to be a more efficient and desirable path towards that function.

We have been indoctrinated with the premise that those who ignore history are doomed to repeat it. The flip side of this is that history reinforces the biases of the winners, who happen to know their history and how to use that to their advantage. The winners of western civilization have a perspective that the same civilized systems empowering them can mitigate the flaws of humanity.

Out of the three distinct perspectives of the social contract that came out of the Enlightenment (Entry #10), Rousseau's most favorable view of humanity was least championed by the winners of history. The Hobbesian perspective of morally flawed humanity empowers authoritarians as winners. The Lockean perspective of humanity needing guidance empowers representatives as winners. Rousseau's perspective would empower public servants responsible for facilitating direct participation.

The Hobbesian perspective draws a parallel with Plato's view of philosopher-kings applying reason to determine what is wise and virtuous for society.[60] The obvious flaw with this view is that authoritarians who thirst for power are least likely to be virtuous. The Lockean perspective reinforces use of dialectic reasoning by the "best and brightest" folks providing arguments and counter arguments to draw ever closer to truth and wisdom. Dialectic reasoning falls apart as a pathway towards wisdom if all sides share the same bias, as is the case with the winners of history. The worst case occurs when the different sides of a dialectic process are corrupted by the same thirst for power or wealth.

The ten year *Unenlightened Wisdom Project* sides with Rousseau's perspective, based upon an empirical foundation of neuroscience and ethnography. Behaviors that physiologically enhance brain health, such as being social and positive, provide a favorable view of humanity. The ethnographic study of small band societies reveal them to be more social and positive than the mass societies that define civilizations. This humanitarian perspective based on the wisdom of science provides hope that collective wisdom of an electorate is both possible and desirable.

With anything gone wrong, the winners of history conditions society to blame people rather than the system that helped to make them winners. We are to focus on corruptible people rather than the corrupting system. The main obstacle to overcome for collective wisdom is thus not the flaws of humanity, but rather the perspective of the winners. Participatory government provides

---

[60] Plato. (1946). *The Republic*. (B. Jowett, Trans.). Fine Editions Press.

a means to overcome this obstacle, when such participation is possible in the context of a nation state.

Entry #27 : Participation and Wisdom

Elections are a key vehicle for shifting blame from a corrupting system onto an electorate allegedly too flawed or too apathetic. Various voter suppression tactics and misleading news systems prevent us from knowing what the "flawed" electorate really wants, at least for close elections. Voter apathy could mean either that the system works well for the electorate as a whole, or has failed miserably to the extent of creating cynicism. After all, at the national level the electorate is voting on who decides issues for them, never participating in the decisions themselves.

Complexity and hierarchy prevents governments of mass societies from being mainly participatory; at best they might aspire to a participatory branch. In keeping with the theme of checks and balances between branches, the intuitive function of a participatory branch would be to devise the rules that limit corruption and increase accountability from the branches that are not participatory. Issues such as term limits, campaign finance and qualified immunity likely have a different outcome if subjected to a collective wisdom process, rather than the dialectic reasoning of representative and/or authoritarian parties and branches.

In the absence of a participatory branch that provides a check and balance to other branches, might we instead provide Amendments to the Constitution towards that end? In addition to a Bill of Rights for the electorate, might there be as well a Bill of Accountability for representatives and authoritarians? Might there be a Bill of Responsibilities for corporations whose very existence depends on suckling the government teat, contrary to free market ideals?

Indeed, while even a militia can exist privately, a for profit corporation cannot. Also, while responsibility to others enhances brain health, such responsibility can hurt the bottom line for shareholder capitalism. Human nature has a built in responsibility component if not undermined by civilized pandering and punditry; corporations as effective wards of the state instead require governments to administer parental guidance to check their greed, often with petulant defiance on their part. Along with other factors, maximizing for profit corporate health minimizes human health.

Unfortunately, amending the Constitution ultimately calls for representative and/or authoritarian action, not participatory. Accountability and responsibility Amendments do not stand a chance of passage through current Constitutional rules. At best we might hope for direct participation remedies similar to the referendum process in the states.

Even if we could surmount the current odds against amending the Constitution or national referendums occurring, the electorate faces yet another challenge for holding leaders accountable. Can an electorate vote responsibly when their leaders encourage entitlement for what is deserved and resentment for what is undeserved by others? Can participatory government provide collective wisdom in an atmosphere of pandering?

Entry #28: Pandering versus Wisdom

"Marketing" and "pandering" have similar objectives of persuading the undecided. We expect for profit corporations to sell us things we might not otherwise buy; we expect political campaigns to do the same. Both can misinform with their marketing or pandering, thus thwarting the potential wisdom of consumers or voters.

When marketing persuades us to unwisely buy a product, we consider that to be buyer's remorse. Unless the marketer made unkept promises or warranties, the fault of an unwise purchase lies with the buyer. With pandering not even unkept promises matter and no warranties exist, yet the fault of an unwise election still allegedly lies with the voters, not pandering parties or politicians. References to "stupid" or "ignorant" voters is consistent with the "blame the people, not the system" advocacy of those who benefit from the system.

Lies circulate faster than truth on social media, providing another "blame the people" opportunity to indict our gullibility. Yet similar to exorbitant marketing budgets for corporations, engaging people emotionally requires resources. Truth only needs the resources to report; falsehoods need the additional resources to fabricate. Only proper context is necessary to "sell" a truth, which can be supplied along with the reporting; a falsehood requires the resources to replace context with emotional theatre.

One approach to rein in a "pandering campaign" would be to limit campaign resources, constricting the time, money and/or effort needed for pandering to be more effective than reporting the truth. Both the length and costs of our election campaigns are wildly out of proportion with other countries. Even after gaining office, representatives must spend much of their time and effort with continued fundraising for both themselves and their party.

Unfortunately, limiting campaign resources faces the same obstacle as national referendums. We cannot expect our representative and authoritarian leaders to limit the resources of a system that benefits representatives and authoritarians. Supplying contextual information rather than pandering requires leaders with more of a public service orientation than either "the best and brightest" or "strongmen" have.

A twist occurs when we assume successful businessmen are "the best and brightest" we seek for public office. The most successful businessmen run shareholder corporations, which succeed in part by gaming public systems to their private advantage. They also are the most successful at pandering, er, I mean marketing, to get people buying what they are selling. Indeed, Trump published a book called *The Art of the Deal*, which boasts about telling people what they want to hear in order to get what he wants. This happens to be a good description of pamdering.

With our current news climate, representatives and authoritarians do not need pandering to tag successful economic elites as "the best and brightest" for a public office, where they can use their business experience to make the best use of insider trading. Corporate funded think tanks and mainstream media provide experts that calmly and rationally explain why the economic policies best for corporations, shareholders and a global investment economy are best for America. We call such experts pundits.

Entry #29: Punditry versus Wisdom

As a multidisciplinary STEM academic I studied how natural systems work. Concepts such as structure and function, homeostasis and causation versus correlation apply just as well to understanding social systems. Unfortunately, many social scientists who serve as media pundits do not seem to agree.

Mainstream punditry consistently refers to our national government as a democracy, in contradiction to Rousseau's participatory function and Lincoln's "by the people" structure. Pundits point to peaceful transfers of power, free and fair elections, and checks and balances between branches as necessary conditions for democracy. Putting aside our shortcomings with each of these conditions, all of them together still are not sufficient for gaining collective wisdom "by the people."

Mainstream punditry compounds this misleading branding when citing clear examples of groupthink as populism. Since we wish the government to make wise decisions, this implies that democracy has a populist people problem. If this be true then the function of democracy was never wise rule, but rather to throw a bone of "liberty" to an electorate, with mitigations for the folly that might occasionally result. Yet freedom without responsibility, including the responsibility to make informed decisions, is really indulgence instead, the type of "freedom" that fuels pandering.

Authoritarian government is wise if the leaders are wise, an improbable result given the corruption and lack of accountability with unchecked power. Representative government is allegedly wise through the dialectic process of thesis and antithesis, policy and counter policy, to arrive at a synthesis of wisdom. This process falls short of wisdom when all sides share the same bias, such as the biases of representatives in regards to a political system that benefits representatives.

Participatory government falls short of collective wisdom when replaced by groupthink. Yet groupthink is a systemic problem, not a people problem, that requires changes to mainstream punditry. We will not remedy the ongoing systemic problems of the status quo by implementing democracy if we are led to believe we already have one. Issues such as the absence of national referendums or the presence of absurdly complex tax codes will remain out of focus from mainstream punditry, as will a critical look at our two party system.

Entry #30: Parties versus Wisdom

Political parties are a type of interest group, indeed, the most influential interest groups in our country. As such they are the greatest cause of groupthink through their party platforms and pandering. Our Founding Fathers instinctively knew political parties to be a problem (Entry #11), yet they are here to stay. How, then, do we mitigate the problem of party groupthink?

The *Unenlightened Wisdom Project* journeys from a starting point of brain health towards a destination of democracy over a period of ten years. Countries with better brain health, emotional health and happiness than ours tend to have multiple parties and coalition governments. Multiple parties provide the accountability that a potentially authoritarian government depending wholly on wise leaders or constitutions would lack. Coalitions provide accountability that a winner-take-all, representative government would lack.

Let us recognize the contrasting party platforms for what they are as of the year 2024. Democrats want to protect the status quo of a two party system. We have systemic political, economic and health problems associated with this status quo, but for profit corporations benefit from this system and mainstream media bias reflects that. The dominating MAGA branch of Republicans currently challenge the status quo with effectively a one party solution. Working to their advantage has been the emergence of a bad faith news media system that will promote proven falsehoods unless coerced otherwise.

Neither party advocates for multiple parties nor the coalition government associated with less wealth disparity and better health outcomes in other countries. We cannot assume the representatives/authoritarians of either party ever will. A more feasible solution to the problems of partisanship and bipartisanship would be nonpartisanship, considering that we now have over 50% more unaffiliated voters in the electorate than members of either party.[61] At the least a nonpartisan approach aligns more with the Constitution's original intent.

Unaffiliated voters react against the two parties, but many are still influenced by the pandering and punditry that leads us away from democracy and collective wisdom. "Ignorant," "stupid," and/or "narcissistic" people still draw the ire of many unaffiliated voters; witness the memes posted by your friends on social media. Rather than reacting negatively to systemic problems currently beyond our control, we need a positive direction towards collective wisdom that can be pursued at a grassroots level, apart from the parties, punditry, pandering and bad faith news media that dominate national politics. Based upon neuroscience and ethnographies of small band societies, a positive direction for either democracy or brain health requires a positive lifestyle.

---

[61] *Party Affiliation.* (2025). Gallup Historical Trends. Retrieved on 05/15/2025 from https://news.gallup.com/poll/15370/party-affiliation.aspx

Entry #31: Positivity and Wisdom

When my wife Cindy was let go from work due to cognitive decline, we turned to our passion of long distance hiking and walked 5,000 miles across the country. I could not share publicly at the time why we were uprooting our lives at this stage. Instead, I gave talks about kindness and community along our route and reported my observations of the same on my Humanity Hiker blog.[62] The website featured the tagline:

"Love kindness. Build community. Believe in humanity."

Loving kindness results from a feeling of either belonging or empathy. Kind acts cement a feeling of belonging with a spirit of general reciprocity. You help a neighbor and someday you know a neighbor will help you, even if not the same neighbor. In response to empathy, kind acts provide a release of biochemicals that enhance brain health, known as helper's high. Of particular note, kindness motivated by empathy is more likely to provide a health benefit when there is no expectation of reciprocity, such as helping complete strangers in need never to be encountered again, as long as the kindness successfully alleviates sorrow or suffering in others.

I observed and reported on how kind acts build caring communities across the country. People with a feeling of belonging seek to take care of their own, regardless of demographic differences. Even if nationally we do not believe the "other" should be helped, we particularly hate to see our own neighbors hungry, homeless or without health care. We will never end hunger and homelessness nationally, but in some local communities (tribes!) these problems have been eliminated.

As strangers in every place we walked I also observed the kindness that results from an empathetic perception of need. One day as we hiked across a Nevada desert during a heat wave all six recreational vehicle travelers we encountered stopped to see how we were doing (oddly enough, we were the only people hiking in the desert during a heat wave). They offered water, food and even money to a seedy looking, middle-aged couple, hiking with heavy packs in the middle of nowhere. Six out of six felt a compulsion to help strangers they knew they would never see again.

I adopted the kindness tagline before our walk across the country, my belief in humanity having grown out of my previous long distance journeys. This belief was reinforced as we met hundreds of strangers who became instant friends in the moment. I explained this phenomenon during my talks to community organizations, schools and churches with the saying: "Expect trouble, find trouble. Expect kindness, find kindness."

The negativity of panderers, pundits and political parties leads us to expect trouble from each other. At best we expect "the other" to be stupid or ignorant, at worst we expect all of us to be

---

[62] The website for the Humanity Hiker blog is https://www.humanityhiker.com/.

morally challenged. We will never change or overcome this onslaught of negativity at the national level, nor will these sources of centralized negativity endorse collective wisdom through participatory government.

Only at the grassroots level can we expect and find abundant kindness from each other. At worst this grassroots focus leads us to build and nurture community. At best we enhance our brain health and provide the first stepping stone towards the democracy that panderers, pundits and parties only pretend we have at the national level.

Grassroots initiatives take time, particularly if they lead to something as broadly sweeping as democratic social systems. This election year journal provides a glimpse of the end goals of the *Unenlightened Wisdom Project.* Subscribe and contribute to this ten year journey, from the positivity that benefits brain health to the democracy that benefits social systems.

ELECTION POST MORTEM

Entry #32: Caveat Emptor!

Punditry is a popular pastime for both sports and politics. Both types of pundits provide opinions on winners or losers to audiences tuning in for extended content. Seldom do sport pundits analyze how the rules of the game affects the outcome; the rules are a given. Seldom do political pundits discuss how systemic conditions affect the outcome of elections; those conditions similarly are a given.

From researching our social systems for decades, resulting in one published work[63] and the current *Unenlightened Wisdom Project*, I studied how and why those in charge of government, as well as segments of academia, condition society to hold people instead of systems responsible. For voting this assumes a caveat emptor (voter beware) in response to whatever politicians or news media are "selling" to the public. We call the pitches of political campaigns "pandering," similar in style to the sales pitches known as marketing campaigns. Much of media punditry cover the impact of political pandering on voters, yet the 2024 election provided a clear example of how the system, not the people, determines the outcome.

Entry #9 of this election year journal covered the three basic types of governance based upon Enlightenment views of human nature and the social contract: authoritarian, representative and participatory. Participatory government as the truest form of democracy requires direct participation from the electorate, such as by state referendums or town hall meetings. For straightforward, personal issues such as reproductive rights, people rely on their own experiences and beliefs to make decisions. For complex issues such as immigration or the economy, or the complexity of how a Presidential candidate will govern, people turn to news sources they trust for guiding their vote. This helps explain the apparent contradiction between a large majority of red states protecting reproductive rights through referendums, while also voting for Trump.

Limited experience creates bias, while expanding the quantity and diversity of experiences facilitates wisdom. This is the reason why wisdom increases with age, but also the principle behind both the scientific method and the highest function of democracy. Referendums aggregate the diversity of experiential biases and intentions of an electorate, thus normalizing all the biases from societal experiences into collective wisdom. Moral intentions can be subjective and fuzzy (thus, terrific fodder for punditry and pandering!), but moral outcomes often can be measured to gauge the wisdom of a referendum.

---

[63] I published *Systems out of Balance: How Misinformation Hurts the Middle Class* in 2009, right before I became a 24/7 caregiver for my wife in cognitive decline. I provided no follow-up to that work until now, as my attention had been diverted towards a more important journey.

Both in our own history and in a global comparison of countries, protecting reproductive rights has the moral outcomes of fewer deaths of the mother, lower child mortality and lower abortion rates.[64] Yes, lower abortion rates. Empirical evidence reveals that countries allowing for greater responsibility and rights of individuals have fewer abortions than countries passing laws to restrict those rights and usurping individual responsibility. Referendums on reproductive rights, as judged by moral outcomes rather than a dialectic of moral intentions, demonstrates the collective wisdom of people directly participating in democracy.

Unfortunately, increased complexity increases the need to depend on news sources rather than personal experiences for making decisions. All news media, like all humanity, have biases. Local media have local biases, unless in reality the stations are centrally owned and controlled, such as with all the local stations owned and controlled by Sinclair Broadcasting.[65] Mainstream media tends to have a corporate bias due to corporate ownership. These biases sometimes misinform and conform with errors of commission and omission, but traditional news sources at least provide the news in good faith. This means they readily retract or correct their investigative reporting when proven wrong, rather than create or echo known and proven investigative falsehoods and propaganda.

Entry #25 described the bad faith news media system[66] that promotes an agenda rather than providing news as their intended purpose. They will not retract or correct falsehoods unless coerced, typically by a lawsuit, and even then will prefer to settle rather than have their bad faith intentions publicly exposed.[67] The results of the 2024 election provided both a litmus test for this system and a measure of its current influence on the electorate.

Polling revealed that in 2024 one third of the population still did not believe Biden was our legitimate President.[68] People with a sense of belonging to their country do not wake up one morning and suddenly decide that our courts and elections cannot be trusted, since none of their own personal experiences would provide validating evidence for such cynicism. Overlooking the substantial evidence that confirmed Biden as President requires herding by news sources. For example, Fox News chose not to air the January 6 committee hearings that included testimony from Trump's aides that he knew the election was legitimate. Fox News and the rest of the bad faith media system instead portrayed the hearings as a politically motivated stunt.

The one third of the electorate that believed the 2020 election was stolen likely voted almost exclusively for Trump. Rounding the vote count down to 150 million for the sake of easy math, if only 45 out of 50 million voters (90%) influenced by bad faith news media voted for Trump, he just needed about 30 out of the 100 million voters (30%) who get their news from good faith

---

[64] Online database "https://worldpopulationreview.com/country-rankings/abortion-rates-by-country."

[65] Online article "https://www.vox.com/2018/4/6/17202824/sinclair-tribune-map."

[66] *Election Campaign Wisdom*, Entry #25: News Media Systems.

[67] Online article "https://apnews.com/article/fox-news-dominion-lawsuit-trial-trump-2020-0ac71f75acfacc52ea80b3e747fb0afe"

[68] Online article https://thehill.com/homenews/campaign/4384619-one-third-of-americans-say-biden-election-illegitimate/"

sources to win the election. Given the diversity of the electorate, requiring 70 out of 100 million (70%) to vote in favor of anything without being herded into groupthink is a bar too high for collective wisdom to prevail.

Trump likely would have won the 2020 election because of the influence of bad faith news media on about one third of the population, had not the pandemic caused much of the electorate to vote according to what they were experiencing, in defiance of the pandering and punditry from the bad faith system. The post pandemic turned the experiential tables back in favor of Trump because of inflation and immigration, two experiential yet complex issues checking all the boxes for emotional pandering (Entry #21). Given this experiential handicap, receiving 70% of votes from the portion of the electorate not herded by bad faith news media reflected a supermajority of support for Harris. Might Harris have tweaked her campaign to achieve one extra percent of voters? Perhaps, but punditry focused on how to better pander to people misses the point.

If punditry shifted away from the behavior of voters and candidates in the present to how systemic factors change over time, caveat emptor no longer applies. The system authoritarians or representatives have created become the target rather than a misguided electorate. Entry #5 of this journal covered how news media changed since the sixties. The seventies provided the pundits, the eighties the expanded venue for punditry, while the nineties founded the bad faith news media. Considering the impact of bad faith news media on election results, there likely was no chance Trump could win if the election was held before the nineties, and even less chance that someone of Trump's flawed character could become a candidate before the opinion driven news of the eighties.

Pundits determined to apply caveat emptor to voters might point to a significant portion of the electorate choosing to trust bad faith news media. Entry #7 described how pundits also mislabel the groupthink caused by bad faith news media as "populism" or "tribalism,"[69] doggedly shifting the responsibility for flawed beliefs from sources that herd an electorate to people who naturally flock to these dubious sources. This fails to account for systemic changes that cause people to trust in news that challenges the status quo.

Whether we call our system of governance participatory, representative, authoritarian or some combination of the three, let us instead simply call that system our status quo. For decades our status quo increased wealth disparity, with additional harmful trends to lifestyles, no matter which party was in control of any branch of government.[70] When pundits refer to our status quo as "democracy," this implies that harmful economic and health trends for decades resulted from this form of government. The logical solution then becomes one that discounts the will of the people and moves further away from democratic principles.

The status quo determines what pundits analyzing voters consider to be moderate, centrist or mainstream views at any point in time. President Dwight Eisenhower was considered to be a

---

[69] *Election Campaign Wisdom*, Entry #7: Confronting Complexity and Conformity.
[70] Describing the political causes and economic consequences of growing wealth disparity for decades was the central thesis for *Systems out of Balance: How Misinformation Hurts the Middle Class*.

moderate Republican in the fifties, while now mainstream news media sometimes labels Senator Bernie Sanders a radical progressive, yet both have a similar economic philosophy (Entry #2). The Eisenhower/Sanders philosophy works well in other advanced countries and would have reduced wealth disparity in ours. If elements of this philosophy such as universal health care were put to a participatory vote at a national level those measures would pass, similar to the reproductive rights referendums at state levels.

An apologetic view of the status quo might claim we aspire to be a democracy, akin to the pursuit of unattainable perfection. Such aspirations still require more than talk or symbolism, occasionally making something happen. For democracy this would mean decreasing the complexity of government when possible, reducing the pandering by campaigns and punditry of news sources, providing contextual information for the electorate and/or encouraging direct participation at the national level. Parties, politicians, pundits and news media advocated none of this in response to the collective wisdom provided by the reproductive rights referendums.

Neither party calls for an expansion of direct participation to manifest true democracy at the national level, nor do they recommend reducing the complexity of a system whose checks and balances have intricate loopholes. Consider what the results of participatory government at the national level might be on issues such as term limits, campaign financing, immunity and other measures to hold authoritarians or representatives accountable. Consider how responsible voters might draw upon their own experiences for voting if tax codes, appropriation bills and governing processes were simplified and easily understood.

We have a system of pandering and punditry that claims caveat emptor for voters, while depriving the electorate of the information and context needed to vote responsibly. Caveat emptor for a true democracy requires reduced complexity, less pandering by politicians (or marketing by corporate funded think tanks), increased contextual information and leaders who become more like public servants than strongmen or "the best and brightest." Such systemic changes likely will have to be a grassroots movement resistant to the groupthink of political parties, so be prepared when mainstream punditry disparages such a movement as populism.

www.ingramcontent.com/pod-product-compliance
Lightning Source LLC
Chambersburg PA
CBHW081724270326
41933CB00017B/3294